DESIGNERS ON DESIGNERS

INTERIOR: ROBERTO PEREGALLI AND LAURA SARTORI RIMINI. PHOTO: MASSIMO LISTRI.

Designers
on
Designers

THE INSPIRATION BEHIND GREAT INTERIORS

~

Susan Gray

MCGRAW-HILL
New York   Chicago   San Francisco   Lisbon   London   Madrid
Mexico City   Milan   New Delhi   San Juan   Seoul
Singapore   Sydney   Toronto

The McGraw·Hill Companies

Library of Congress Cataloging-in-Publication Data

Gray, Susan (Susan Kimberly)
  Designers on designers : the inspiration behind great interiors / Susan Gray.
    p. cm.
  Includes index.
  ISBN 0-07-142160-2 (alk. paper)
    1. Interior decoration—History—20th century.   2. Interior decorators—Psychology.
  I. Title.

  NK1980.G73 2003
  747—dc21   2003056211

1 2 3 4 5 6 7 8 9 0   DOC/DOC   0 1 0 9 8 7 6 5 4 3

ISBN 0-07-142160-2

The sponsoring editor for this book was Cary Sullivan and the production supervisor was Sherri Souffrance. It was set in Goudy Old Style by North Market Street Graphics. The art director for the cover was Margaret Webster-Shapiro.

Printed and bound by RR Donnelley.

This book was printed on acid-free paper.

McGraw-Hill books are available at special quantity discounts to use as premiums and sales promotions, or for use in corporate training programs. For more information, please write to the Director of Special Sales, Professional Publishing, McGraw-Hill, Two Penn Plaza, New York, NY 10121-2298. Or contact your local bookstore.

CONTENTS

—

FOREWORD

by Albert Hadley

What makes Sammy run? Curiosity? Curiosity, in this case, prompts our investigation into the lives of contemporary designers as we attempt to fathom what influences and circumstances have motivated performance in their quest for accomplishment.

In this beautiful and well-documented book, we are brought into close proximity, in a very personal and entertaining manner, with a group of star performers whose focus is on the creation of exemplary interiors. In each case we are given a totally energizing run—a run fraught with history, philosophy, and often delectable anecdotes. The writers share with us their individual points of view with honesty, charm, and even sometimes wicked wit!

In essence, each story is a tribute to a mentor who has inspired and often guided the writer's individual professional pursuits. But what exactly is a mentor? From Greek mythology one learns that Mentor was a great teacher. He was Odysseus's wise and trusted counselor, under whose disguise Athena became the guardian and teacher of Telemachus. From this fabled name comes the term *mentor*. To this day, mentors are great teachers, oftentimes unaware of their influence. They are purveyors of a determined philosophy—a point of view, if you will.

Great teachers, great influences, come in many guises. Sometimes even a place or a movement can become the starting signal. From a mentor, in any arena, one gleans knowledge and inspiration, which are the keys to creative production in the development of one's own personal expression. Let us note that knowledge and inspiration are quite different from slavish adherence to the source. Such august teachers require no copybooks!

The assembled essays in *Designers on Designers* are fascinating and telling reflections that reveal a world of discriminating taste, beauty, and a quality of life that far surpasses the ordinary. Each designer's story holds one's attention and is a source of revelation and delight as we are made privy to the aesthetic influences in the lives of these remarkable, creative, talented, and accomplished artists.

Susan Gray is to be congratulated and applauded for bringing forth this stellar cast for our own erudite pleasure.

Albert Hadley

ACKNOWLEDGMENTS

—

Vera Paulsen (my mother), Joanne Wang (my superb agent), Lynne King, Diane de la Begassiere, Christine Biddle, Joan Brunskill, Erica Disch, Charles Evans, Christy Brown, Cheryl Gray, Michael Graves, Caroline Hancock, Michael Klingher, Ray Krell, Carol Leroy, Celeste Long, Marta Levisman, Felix Marcilhac, Chappy Morris, Collins Munro, Linda Munson, Peter Napolitano, Mitchell Owens, Galerie Du Passage/Pierre Passebon/ Nathalie Peters, Mark Perera, Mo Teitelbaum, Robert Torday, Jamie Wyeth.

Condé Nast: Leigh Montville, Michael Stier, Florence Palomo.

McGraw-Hill: Cary Sullivan, Elizabeth Schacht, Cathy Markoff, Margaret Webster-Shapiro, Tom Kowalczyk, Mike Hays, David Fogarty, Scott Grillo, Steve Chapman, Sherri Souffrance, John Gerard.

North Market Street Graphics: Carol Olena, Stephanie Landis, Anne DeLozier, Vicki Dawes, Jan Bedger.

Carol Ingram, Marilyn and Martin Tully, Beverly Adler, David Adler, David Adler Cultural Center, Melissa Althen, ARS (Janet Hicks, Cristin O'Keefe Aptowicz), Leslie Banker, Camille Berthelot, Terry Bird, Jill Bloomer, Eric C. Bongartz, Lee Bowman, Rachel Brishoual, Sally Ann Calabrese, Jose Antonio Carlino, Laura Cattano, John Clausen, Mary Caroline

Acknowledgments

Clifton, Tomas Clusellas, Christine Cordazzo, Debra Crusan, Billy Cunningham, Robin Cunningham, David Deatherage, Amanda Dreyer, Marian Earnest, the Fiorella family, Michael Frank, the Gray family, Joseph Guidera, Alexa and Duane Hampton, John M. Hall, Martin Harvey, Wanda Myers Hines, Wendy Hurlock, Mark Kelly, Lisetta Koe, Pam Kueber, Massimo Listri, Geoff Lung, Susan Manne, Maureen Martin, Brooke Mason, Judi McKee for Julius Shulman, Anastasia Mikliaeva, Pilar Molyneux, Linda and Julio Montes, Jim Murphy, Mitchell Owen, Susan Pabon, Susan Palmer, Paulette Pascarella, Charles Patteson, Claudia Pierrottet, Nancy Porter, Tracey Winn Pruzan, Greg Richardson, Kim Sargent, Laura Sartori Rimini, Nancy Romeu, Cynthia Sanford, Keith Shore, Stella Calvert-Smith, Haley Stevenson, Jill Tasta, Les Thompson, Martha Thorne, Lynn Davis-Trier, Tevfik Unver, John Vaughan, Peter Vitale, Elle Wrench, and Nellie Xinos.

DESIGNERS ON DESIGNERS

Pamela S. Banker

~ on ~

SIR JOHN SOANE

I can't remember exactly when I first heard of Sir John Soane, but it was many years ago in my student days, and initially his was just a name that I tucked away in my mental file of brilliant architects. About 20 years ago I started a real, tangible file that has grown with articles on Soane and with information I received from the Sir John Soane's Museum at 13 Lincoln's Inn Field in London. Soane's house, which is now a museum, is unlike any interior I had ever seen before; the design and the use of light and color were amazing. I was intrigued by Soane's versatility—his ability to design a small gate-keeper's lodge as beautifully as grand country houses, not to mention the Bank of England building. But it was not until I actually went to the museum that I fully experienced the brilliance of Sir John Soane.

It was in the early spring about 15 years ago that I took a short trip to London with the purpose of going to the museum. It was my first visit. Instead of the hour or two I expected to stay, I was there for half a day. While the photographs of the house that I had seen were certainly good, they didn't begin to do justice to the real thing. I was struck by the use of color: rich ochres and warm colors throughout, a dining room painted red with forest green trim. The house was alive with patterned wood floors and architectural detail on built-in cabinets. The Georgian period and look has always been a huge influence for me, but this was just something else, something different, intriguing, and inviting.

The phrase *ahead of his time* often comes up when describing Sir John Soane's work. He was active toward the end of the Georgian era and at the advent of the Regency. (His dates are 1753 to 1837.) The ideas at the time regarding scale and majestic spaces were changing, and Soane was at the forefront of that change. He was well versed in classical architecture and took inspiration from buildings he saw during his grand tour in Italy from 1778 to 1780. His brilliance partially stems from the fact that he didn't just follow the prescribed dictates of the classics and the fashions of the time, but rather he was inspired by all he saw around him while coming up with his own interpretations. The genius of Sir John Soane is that almost 200 years after he finished his house, toward the

PREVIOUS SPREAD: *The Library and Dining Room are treated as one room separated by projecting bookcases and an archway with three segments. The curves in the archway are echoed over the bookcases and windows. Soane used mirrors over the fireplace and between the windows and also in the recesses above the bookcases to reflect the arches and the ceiling. The deep red and forest green paint is an example of his strong use of color.*

end of his life, we can still go there and marvel at how unique it is.

Besides the use of color, I was bowled over by Soane's use of light and sources of light. In different rooms throughout the house there are convex circular mirrors mounted on domed ceilings and archways. While standing in the dining room I looked up into one of the convex mirrors and saw myself, tiny in the middle, with the expanse of the room growing around me. These mirrors keep light on its toes, moving and bouncing, and are also an interesting design element unto themselves. They are functional, practical, and wonderfully decorative. The house is designed to make the most of natural light. In the picture room are clerestory windows, and throughout the house are skylights in the most unexpected places flooding light into rooms that would otherwise be dark during the day. At least one sizable mirror is hung in many of the rooms, reflecting natural light during the day and lamplight in the evenings. All this thought to lighting is brilliant, making the house alive and vibrant; it could never become old and dusty with the activity of constantly changing light pulsing through it.

The scale of the house at Lincoln's Inn Field is small, unlike so many grand estates of the time, but the sense of space is tremendous—not necessarily in its largeness but in its fullness. Besides being a great architect, Sir John Soane was a great collector, and the house at Lincoln's Inn Field still holds his various collections of

The domed ceiling of the Breakfast Parlour with intricate ornamental beading is a characteristic example of Soane's style. In 1835 Soane described the Breakfast Parlour: "In the centre rises a spherical ceiling, springing from four segmental arches, supported by the same number of pilasters, forming a rich canopy. The spandrels of the dome and the soffits of the arches are decorated with a number of mirrors. In the dome is an octangular lantern-light, enriched with eight Scriptural subjects in painted glass. At the north and south ends of the room are skylights, which diffuse strong lights over the several Architectural and other works decorating the walls . . ."

everything from paintings by Hogarth to thousands of architectural drawings from the office of Robert and James Adam and hundreds of architectural fragments, casts, and sculptures. The house could very well have ended up feel-

The Picture Room contains works by Hogarth, Canaletto, Turner, and others. The pictures are hung on both sides of wings that swing open and can be latched closed. The detailing in the dado and the paneling of the walls adds interest. Clerestory windows bring light into the room.

ing crammed. This is not the case, though, because there is an order that prevents it from being cluttered. Also, the nature of a collection is that there is a theme. We are not distracted by many little unrelated things throughout the house, but can see the many things as part of a larger whole. Sir John Soane displayed his collections in such a way that they become a part of the integral design of the house. In the Picture Room, there are wings on the wall with paintings hung on both sides. These wings hinge and can be opened to view the paintings on two sides or secured shut. There are stone busts on shelves built high near the ceiling in a hallway, and there are statues on shelves projecting from the wall above a bookcase. These shelves seem to be built for the express purpose of holding the exact statues that rest on them. Everything seems to have a place in this house.

Every space, every inch of the house, has a purpose. A flat plane isn't a flat plane simply because it's not being used; it is a part of the overall design of the space. In what is called the Loggia, off of the drawing room, there is a wooden shelf in a niche where an architectural fragment is placed. This shelf serves the purpose of supporting the niche. The wood tones of the shelf match the floor and add a touch of color to the wall. But what I love about it is that, built into the shelf, is a small drawer with two simple wooden knobs. That drawer was probably quite useful.

There is wonderful book storage all over the house, not just in the library. In the Breakfast

Parlour there are shelves built into the deep walls. In the South Drawing Room there are, most unexpectedly, bookshelves built into the reveals of the windows. The walls are about two feet deep so that 10 or more books can fit into the cross section. Distributing the book collection throughout the house makes it cozy; it adds continuity.

Sir John Soane's incredible use of detail is what kept me in the museum for so long that day. The domed ceiling of the Breakfast Parlour has ornamental beading that is simply perfect right there. In the Picture Room every door has wonderful brass knobs and fasteners, and the ebony inlay in the dado is not too busy or too much but just pleasing to the eye. The mounts on drawers and doors throughout the house are just right, the perfect proportion, not too small and timid and not too big. Taking note of all this reinforced for me the importance of detail in design.

In a New York dining room that I designed for a client some years ago, I created a Gothic theme and took some inspiration from Sir John Soane. There are strong colors—yellow walls with red and blue accents—throughout the room. There is detail on all the furniture: a painted cabinet is elaborately carved, there is egg-and-dart detail around the top of the dining table, and Gothic-style chairs have pointed seat backs and are covered in a bold tapestry fabric. Also, in this room there is a fine collection of blue-and-white delft pottery that is displayed in the cabinet, on the mantel, hanging on the walls

PHOTO: KEITH SCOTT MORTON © *HOUSE & GARDEN*/THE CONDE NAST PUBLICATIONS, LTD.

A New York entryway by Banker with bold stripes and a swagged border on the walls. To the left is a collection of hats on a Georgian mahogany hat and umbrella stand. To the right are two antique painted Italian chairs and on the front door a knocker with bold proportions to complement the scale of the stripes on the walls.

mounted on brackets, and even on the tabletops. I made a point of distributing the collection around the room and making it a part of the overall design.

Also inspiring at the Sir John Soane's Museum is that the rather small entrance hall is so inviting and interesting. This is something I consider in my own work. An entrance hall that I designed, also in New York, has bold black-and-white striped wall covering and a mahogany hat rack with a collection of hats and umbrellas,

A New York City dining room by Pamela Banker with a Gothic theme. The collection of antique blue-and-white delftware is distributed throughout the room. Decorative detail is found in the raised spheres around the top of the dining table, in the pinnacles and recessed panels of the antique glazed bookcase, and in the points of the pelmet that echo the shape of the chairs.

all of which make a strong statement and create an engaging first impression that draws one beyond and into the further interior. Again, a collection—whether it be delft or Audubons or hats and umbrellas—is wonderful to work with as it adds so much to a room.

When designing a country dining room on Long Island a few years ago, I used a rich red color on the walls and put in a clear pine mantel with limewood hand carvings by David Esterly. The wood and detail of the mantel and the patterned oak flooring in the room give it warmth. The dining room has light flowing in from three directions through panes of glass in French doors and over doors, which adds much to the room. I made sure not to obstruct the windows, but to let light pour in.

That first visit to the Sir John Soane's Museum made a tremendous impression. For any architecturally minded person, the genius of the man is overwhelming. Since then I have stopped back periodically for inspiration. Each time I am amazed and impressed by the colors, the lighting, the attention to detail, and the way that every inch of space counts. I am also thankful each time I visit that the house has been so well preserved and that Sir John Soane had the foresight in 1833 to establish it as a museum. I read once that in his lifetime Soane worked on over 300 buildings. (Two of his most famous commissions, the Palace of Westminster and the Bank of England, no longer are standing.) I am reminded of the great responsibility we all share in ensuring that great works of art and architecture are safely cared for so that future generations will be able to see them for themselves and learn from great examples of design and execution.

When I can't get to London but need a bit of inspiration, there is a beautiful publication entitled *Sir John Soane's Museum, London* (Ernst Wasmuth Verlag, 1994) that I flip through. Each time I notice something new, a detail here or there. For

PHOTO: ALEC HEMER©

A dining room on Long Island, New York by Pamela Banker with bold red painted walls. The light floods in through the French doors with transoms above. The hand-carved wood mantle by David Esterly and herringbone-patterned wood floor add texture, warmth, and interest to the room. On the mantel are two Wedgwood basalt vases. The dining chairs are Regency and have delicate proportions typical of the style.

anyone who has just tucked the name Sir John Soane away in a mental file of brilliant architects, I recommend a book such as this highly. And for anyone who has only seen photographs of the museum and who is interested in design, no mat-

ter whether traditional or the most contemporary, I would recommend a visit to the museum if it's possible. Although it's not an enormous space, remember to allow enough time to see it all.

Royère's Cinema privé du Shah d'Iran, 1958. A recreational space treated with an almost official touch, suitable to the client's royal position; we can only guess what the color scheme was.

Mattia Bonetti

~ *on* ~

JEAN ROYÈRE

Translation by Irene Lihau N'Kanza

It is strangely interesting to decipher and analyze people, images, places, odors, and sounds that have preceded us and that, in conscious or unconscious ways, exercise an influence on all aspects of our personality. As far as I am concerned, the sources of inspiration are assuredly plentiful. Personally, I feel assailed by innumerable memories and images that come back to the surface one by one, or sink to more profoundly submerged strata without ever completely disappearing. Instead, they crossbreed with one another, giving birth to a new style.

To me, the revelation of Jean Royère's work goes back to the year 1989 when the Galerie Alan 1930 in Paris asked me if I were interested in designing the setting of the first of the numerous retrospective exhibitions that have since been dedicated to Royère. When I saw the numerous items that were to be exhibited, I felt something familiar, as they had a strong correspondence to the ones that I myself have created in the past. The exhibition comprised only a dozen items, each equally important for its formal and conceptual value. One could therefore see the famous "Boules" canapés and couches, the low "Flaques" tables made with metal or with straw marquetry, and a "Liane" wall lamp.

The exhibition's budget was limited, so I opted for a rustic simplicity that seemed to suit the furniture of Jean Royère. I desired to

Royère's boudoir presente au Salon des Artistes Decorateurs, 1939. This is one of Royère's most feminine and hysterical works, full of humor: is it the boudoir of a lady, an artist, a whore?

upgrade the items by discreetly standing in the background.

Pebbles of all sizes were lacquered in black and served to define the horizontal spaces and floors, while the verticals of the side and main walls were hung with natural raffia and painted with large regular black stripes.

It goes without saying that I had already worked with these materials either for furniture and objects or for elements of decoration. My previous creations included stones or rocks (both real and false), straw, and, of course, lots of wrought iron.

I am writing all of this in preamble to explain and justify what to me is not a trite copy but rather a profound observation of another designer's work, through which I sometimes find a comforting communion. This communion

Hall d'un Chalet à Megève, 1953–1956; crayon de graphite et gouache. A typical Royère interior with a "Boule" couch, a "Flaque" coffee table, and "Liane" wall lamp; the fireplace plays the leading role and the colors are courageous.

enables me as well to apply formulas that by their very nature belong to everyone. The sources of inspiration are plentiful, from all periods and places in the world, sometimes mixed and never obediently following common sense.

There is in Jean Royère's style a trait I share that seems essential to me: an almost obsessive perseverance in the utilization of certain shapes, colors, and materials that renders him fascinating, unique, personal, and in the vanguard.

Chambre à coucher pour M.elle Alexandra Pastor à Paris

Chambre-à-coucher pour M.elle Alexandra Pastor, à Paris

Mrs. Paster's bedroom was based on the young girl's wishes: daisies in wrought iron, ceramic, embroideries, and so on, as designed by Bonetti.

THE SHAPES

Royère uses shapes that are straight or curved, often juxtaposed, basic without by any means being dry or sterile; I would even add that a certain "animal- and vegetable-like inspiration" may be sensed in filigree, resulting in a sane and naive sensuality. Royère's shapes are full, massive, and at times heavy; or they may be empty, sinuous, and light. They pass without complexities from a square to a circle, traversing through the oval to end up at last in a delirium of filaments and organic ellipses.

THE MATERIALS

Traditional, modern and innovative, rich and modest, Jean Royère has exuded audacity while always maintaining casualness and freedom. He has treated and used his materials luxuriously or poorly. Metal tubes and wood may be covered with gold leaf or neatly smeared and color washed with paint.

THE COLORS

Royère's palette oscillates between natural tones and frank, vivid colors, with now and then a joyful and playful range of complementary colors. The mixture of fabric with color is also identifiable, unexpected, and surprising: in the drawer chest "Oeufs," for example, the ash blond natural squared caisson is embedded in a curved structure covered by a collar of blue velvet plush!

Usually sober enough, Royère allows himself to go at times to figurative delusions with flowery

MATTIA BONETTI, 1996.

The "young people's (teenagers')" quarters in the Pastor Paris pied-à-terre as designed by Mattia Bonetti has an almost pop feeling, although elegant and casual.

or geometric motifs hung on the walls, turning themselves around on ceilings to unfurl on simple curtains. Similar to a ritornello, stripes, grid patterns, and dots reappear everywhere—printed, sculpted, and hollowed out on all types of props. More rarely, shapes borrowed from nature—flowers, foliage, stars, and shells—add to the somewhat boring order a childish, cheerful touch.

Today, we view Jean Royère's work through series of photographs—for the most part in black and white but at times in color—or through beautiful drawings evocative of a total look. And though the scale of his projects sometimes exceeds their realization, we are never disappointed by the end result. His great talent is to make the serious cohabit with a humor that

Sir Po Shing and Lady Helen Woo's drawing room by Mattia Bonetti in central Hong Kong, 2002. Irregularly striped white and yellow gold leaf walls; butterfly-shaped coffee tables that give the color scheme to the room; every single item has been exclusively designed and made for the house.

borders on delirium at times. We are plunged into a universe of cartoons, movies, and fair stalls where one does not distinguish between the provisional and the permanent, between infancy and adulthood, between the spirit of small provincial bourgeois and the greatness worthy of the Shah of Iran (who was incidentally a client of Royère's). In a phrase, what moves me and makes me laugh in Jean Royère's work is the absence of snobbery.

What I furthermore appreciate in the work of Jean Royère is its entire suitability and

A Mattia Bonetti design for a Hong Kong interior. Looking from the foyer into the living area, the blue bar is on the right.

appropriateness for his time. In his interiors the furniture, objects, and artworks are always contemporary. He designed his era and contributed in defining it with a gesture and a concept that go well beyond interior decoration. For all of these reasons, his body of work will continue to influence me as well as other creative spirits.

The living room of Diana Vreeland, by Billy Baldwin, known as the "red garden of hell."

Thomas Britt

~ on ~

BILLY BALDWIN

Growing up in Kansas City, Missouri, I was exposed to decorating and antiques at a very tender age by my mother and grandmother. Later I managed to meet and scrutinize the work of the local leading decorators: Peggy Sloane, Altaire and Crawley, Lucy Drage, and Frederick Fender. Fender was in every way, shape, and form a true artist. He created and carved a pair of mirror frames based on the work of Thomas Chippendale, the famous eighteenth-century cabinetmaker and designer. He also taught me how to make marbleized paper. There was also Ester Bushmann, an antiques dealer and party planner, who created the wonderful large-scale rooms and gardens, all so extraordinary it paralleled only the grand designs in Paris. Then there was the firm Melang (parallel to Reny in New York today), which created the greatest fantasies for parties both indoors and in gardens with iron candelabra and epergnes that held candles under tented lamp chimneys dyed in brilliant colors to match the occasion. I thank God today these designers taught me their formulas.

While scouring my mother's issues of *House & Garden*, I came across a living room designed by Bill Pahlmann and fell in love with his work. Pahlmann, a preeminent twentieth-century designer, was a master of creating rooms with great atmosphere by using low-luster or flat paint in

Cole Porter's library by Billy Baldwin in Waldorf Towers; lacquered walls made to look like tortoiseshell; signature brass bookshelves; furniture in beige leather.

covered in python skin. There was a pair of deep, comfortable sofas in green leather, offset by woven shades by Dorothy Libes, a dominant textile designer of the mid-twentieth century. At age 13, I promptly did my own bedroom to emulate the color and atmosphere.

Then there was the ultimate high-fantasy trip with Tony Duquette's house in Beverly Hills. Over the pair of front doors were tiny pyramids in green verdigris bronze, and the doors were flanked by a pair of tall obelisks made of wire mesh, capped with 3-D sunbursts embossed on the wall. The doors opened into a trompe l'oeil hall, with a fantastic meuble—a dark green secretary adorned with seashells, pieces of mirrors, fake emeralds, blackamoors, and dancing sprites that was originally made for Elsie de Wolfe and her friend Lady Mendel.

In 1951 there was an enormous report in *Vogue* magazine of Carlos de Beistegui's ephemeral ball at his Palazzo Labia in Venice. The Palazzo contained the renowned Tiepolo fresco *The Banquet of Cleopatra*. I loved de Beistegui's style in grand scale; there was always a great deal of fantasy injected, whether it be the Palazzo Labia in Venice; his Parisian Corbusier penthouse, where Salvador Dali helped create a surrealistic terrace on the roof; or his Chateau de Groussay, which was an eighteenth-century chateau outside of Paris that was filled with fake and real antiques. I marveled at and studied everything.

At the same period, I loved the work of Van Day Truex, Billy Baldwin, and Frances Elkins.

deeply muted colors. This living room was no exception. On the deeply hued walls, Pahlmann added a grouping of antiques and contemporary paintings that soared to the ceiling. Flanked by a pair of gilt wood Louis XVI chairs done in turquoise leather was a TV and stereo cabinet

Fifth Avenue residence, New York City. A living room where we used two different fabrics you wouldn't normally select together. They played off one another so beautifully. It has the same smooth jazz feeling as the Matisse lithographs.

All three were the epitomes of classic twentieth-century decoration—edited, stylish, chic, and traditional in a contemporary way, creating three highly individual styles that paralleled one another. Of the three, Billy Baldwin was my favorite.

From 1946 to 1955 Billy Baldwin transformed his Amster Yard apartment (a divine courtyard on 49th Street between Second and Third Avenues) three times by changing only the color. In 1946 the apartment's walls were lacquered in dark green gardenia leaf paint.

The slipcovered furniture was in a dark green textured silk and the curtains were an emerald silk. In 1951 the walls were painted white, with yellow satin on the furniture and a brilliant yellow Siamese silk for the curtains. A brush-and-ink Matisse hung in the bedroom and a Spanish still life with icy red apples hung above the sofa in the living room. Then in 1955, the apartment was again transformed by the use of color. The entire room was covered in white brocade, the walls were painted white, the Louis XV armchair was covered in creamy

Fifth Avenue residence, New York City. In this small and cozy library, we left the window bare so the view of Central Park would act as illuminated art and a focal point. We added classical pilasters and trims to existing bookcases that were plain and contemporary, and the effect was spectacular.

brown velvet, and the table was covered to the floor with yards of brown satin. An English painting of hounds hung above the couch in the living room. Billy Baldwin was my idol. His style was always just right, no matter what color!

At the same time, I saw in a magazine a layout where Van Day Truex had designed a room with aubergine walls covered with pictures, matchstick shades, and bare wood floors. I loved it! McMillen had installed polished floors in an incredible living room in St. Louis. Elkins had placed polished floors with two area rugs in a Pebble Beach house. All were great! All rang my Liberty Bell and it cracked!

When I was 18, I enrolled in the Parsons School of Design. I was in ecstasy to be able to actually meet my peers and on my way to realizing my dreams. I attended classes taught by professor Stanley Barrows, the dean of the European School. He taught the periods of seventeenth- and eighteenth-century design in the British Isles and Continental Europe. He would assign us the work of combining elements of traditional and contemporary design. This was similar to what Van Day Truex and Billy Baldwin were doing at the time, which had greatly influenced us all at Parsons. Barrows had a wonderful sense of color and encouraged me to meet Rose Cummings, who was the greatest decorator of high style with her use of superb color and fantasy antiques. The end of my second year was topped off with a grand tour of Europe with Mr. Barrows himself.

But the greatest treat in store for me came one Saturday afternoon after I had graduated from Parsons: Billy Baldwin took four of us on a

PHOTO: ©JAIME ARDILE-ARCE, ORIGINALLY PUBLISHED IN *ARCHITECTURAL DIGEST,* NOVEMBER 1996.

tour, as he knew how much we admired his work. The group included me; Edward Zajak (a classmate and an assistant to Mr. Baldwin); Richard Callahan (another classmate); and my wife, Julie Britt, who was then a fashion editor. We took off to Cole Porter's apartment in the Waldorf Towers: so sublime with the famous dark brown lacquered library with the brass étagères holding all his books. The bergères were in tawny leather similar to the inspired upholstery of Jean-Michel Frank (the great French decorator of the 1930s). The large living room was covered with superb seventeenth-century Chinese wallpaper that had come from Knole, the great English house owned by the famous Sackville family. And how could one ever forget the polished eighteenth-century herringbone parquet Versailles floors with acoustical mud beneath so Mr. Porter could play all his magic on his pair of black lacquered Steinway grand pianos? All of this was put together in a very simple classical way with comfortable upholstery, straight curtains, and contemporary accents combined with magnificent French eighteenth-century furniture that Mr. Porter and his late wife had collected in the 1920s when they were living on the rue Monsieur in Paris. And let's not forget Mr. Porter's bedroom with a red bed and fire-engine-red walls! Great for the great!

We next visited Bill and Babe Paley's Parisian-style cocoon at the St. Regis, with its shirred walls and comfy lounge furniture in a small geometric brown print, all underlined by a sublime Bessarabian rug with a magical chandelier above and a double-faced clock and barometer with blackamoors holding candles. There was also an incredible Gothic mirror that hung on the wall over the sofa.

We went up Park Avenue and next entered the red door to the red garden of Diana Vreeland, who was at the time the fashion editor extraordinaire of *Vogue*. Her living room floor was covered with a red carpet, and almost everything—walls, curtains, and furniture—was covered with the most incredible Persian scarlet chintz fabric that had come from John Fowler's shop in London. The fabric had enormous scarlet flowers on a red background. The dining room walls and banquette were covered in a multicolor striped fabric. There were a pair of tiny slipper chairs from Jansen juxtaposed with a giant deep sofa with sheets of mirrors over it. And there were Vreeland's needlepoint cushions, as well as a needlepoint by the fashion illustrator Bébé Bérard. Mundane furniture on one wall, including bookshelves painted white, combined with ravishing accessories, all permeated by the scent of Riguad candles. It truly was a "red garden of hell"!

We went next to 72nd Street and Madison Avenue, to the apartment of Speed Lamkin. Here was another room with patterned shirred fabric on the walls, except this one had a very long, very low, and very deep banquette in a corner with a shorter ell. The banquette was covered in the same shirred cotton as the walls,

Watercolor rendering of a dining room in a residence in Scarsdale, New York, as designed by Thomas Britt.

giving the room a tent-like feeling. A round dining table with six chairs could be pushed up to the banquette for dining. Mr. Baldwin had placed two French chairs in solid velvet fabric flat against the wall on either side of the fireplace. Then there was a smaller sofa at the other end of the room, with a low lacquered table used for high noon tea. The whole effect was wonderful.

We next went to the Watson Blair apartment, and it was pure Baldwin: ivory walls, and tobacco-brown silk curtains with triple ruffles on the bottom and deep, medium, and shorter lengths overlaying one another. You could see John Fowler's influence here, but it was definitely Baldwin; straight with the flounce at the bottom, like a flamenco skirt. This was combined with a printed cotton, large-scale black-

and-white damask on the lounge furniture; brown leather on French chairs; a Kan Hsi mirror; black Chinese porcelains wired for lamps with gessoed opaque paper shades; polished floors with rare Spanish rugs; and in walked a Tony Duquette fantasy with a splendid pair of Brighton Pavilion brass palm trees complete with small coconuts.

At this point, the cocktail hour was nearing, so Billy whisked us back to his apartment. Here was the famous black-and-gold lacquered Korean screen with a tray on a leather luggage rack for drinks. We sat on the raw Thai silk slipcovered Baldwin settee and slipper chairs and lounged on the great Baldwin sofa set against the wall covered in ecru.

I had already done my first black room with white painted floors when I was 15 years old, so I was both flattered and amused that I could recognize myself in Baldwin's work. Baldwin's use of dark brown walls later became the rage in New York City and elsewhere. It was 40 years ago and one of the most memorable days of my life.

In my own New York City apartment, I modulated curtains like Baldwin's in an all-red room with a seventeenth-century table, chairs, and chest. When Pope John XXIII visited the city in the 1950s, we hung the drapes out of our window for him to bless. When he came down our street, he acknowledged them with a holy wave. Thank God our prayers worked and he recognized us; all thanks to Billy Baldwin!

Later, in my new apartment, I did rooms with shirred walls and created tented rooms for an assistant of mine and one for a client. For our country house, which was built from an eighteenth-century barn, I covered the sofas in winter slipcovers with material that Billy had brought me from Madrid. The material was similar to the big red-patterned fabric that he had used in Diane Vreeland's New York City apartment, only mine had a green background.

I was fascinated with Billy Baldwin's brilliant and offbeat furniture arrangements. When analyzed, they were pure logic, whether they were symmetrical or asymmetrical—whatever variation, they worked. Studying his design principles had a profound effect on me. I consider what I do appropriate for the people I create for—it is all about making people feel wonderful in their homes.

SOURCES

Billy Baldwin, *Billy Baldwin Decorates*. New York: Holt, Rinehart, 1972.

Billy Baldwin, *Billy Baldwin Remembers*. New York: Harcourt Brace Jovanovich, 1974.

Billy Baldwin, Michael Gardine (ed.), *Billy Baldwin: An Autobiography*. Boston: Little, Brown, 1985.

Robert Couturier

~ *on* ~

GERMAIN BOFFRAND, EMILIO TERRY, AND EILEEN GRAY

I t would be both foolish and pretentious for any designer to say his or her creations are totally unique, owing nothing to even a single figure in history. After all, there is nothing that has not existed in some form beforehand. Whether it is a single room or an entire residence with multiple ancillary buildings and vast gardens, the design owes a debt in some way to legendary figures in the pantheon of design.

But too often, we see design that is purely one-dimensional—say, a predictable retelling of the English country house look, a limited pastiche of Art Deco splendor, or a tired variation on contemporary minimalism. How do we react to those imitation Georgian living rooms plied with

Chippendale chests, those recasts of eighteenth-century boiserie, and the like? Well, quite frankly, the response is a kind of boredom. Distilling the principles of pivotal designers is critical; lamely copying their styles should be forbidden.

For me, designing a residence for today is about far more than supplying the requisite doors and chairs—much less the appropriate window treatments—and referencing the past. The process really involves creating a personal universe, one charged with a certain level of emotion. Above all, superlative design communicates a specific presence.

For me, that presence, which ultimately reflects designers of the past on a number of dif-

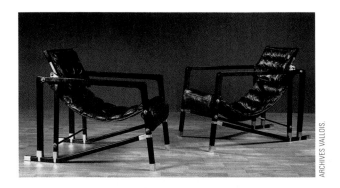

ARCHIVES VALLOIS.

Irish-born designer Eileen Gray's pair of "Transat" chairs in black leather and metal epitomizes a purity of design. Robert Couturier purchased a single copy of these iconic chairs, which were designed in 1925, and it now reposes in his Paris apartment. "This chair was the opposite of all I had known in terms of its totally uncluttered and streamlined design," says Couturier.

ferent levels, should envelope and elevate the inhabitant. After all, great design from a solitary room to an entire chateau makes us quite literally stand up straighter, put a surer foot forward, and ultimately be more engaging. That's the response, the kind of emotional involvement, that I aim for again and again.

PREVIOUS SPREAD: *The legend of Emilio Terry especially rests on his design of this library in Charles de Beistegui's widely acclaimed Chateau de Groussay. There may be hundreds of textures and tonalities amidst this room filled with treasures from the decorative arts, yet overall the room is underscored with comfort, warmth, and wisdom. Robert Couturier remembers with fondness many an afternoon spent in this library.*

I gleaned that lesson on the essence of design at the tender age of seven. My mother had taken me for a visit to Germain Boffrand's Hôtel de Soubise (completed in the late 1730s and now the Archives Nationales), considered by architectural historians one of the most important manifestations of the rococo style. Even then, though my days were consumed with dreary school texts and only lightened by creating new structures out of ubiquitous Legos, I was bowled over by Boffrand's fanciful design and sensed its uniqueness. Yes, it made me stand up straighter, and my mind was amused, titillated, and charmed.

Boffrand (1667–1754), that storied Paris architect who stepped out of the rigorous discipline and rigid classicism of the ancien régime, went on to create the lightness of the rococo. This Parisian literally designed everything from the sumptuous fabrics to exquisite candelabra, but, more important, he totally reinterpreted the very architecture of his period as a sculptural statement par excellence.

On the one hand, Boffrand's octagonal room is born of the eighteenth-century sense of order, geometry, and logic handed down by Descartes. Each of the eight sections of the room is clearly delineated. Yet, on the other hand, this lavish salon is the height of rococo— all consuming yet with a lightness of touch. Of course, there are the distinctive touches of white and gold, the swooning S-shaped curves; the naturalistic motifs—sprigs of flowers; and the imaginative plasterwork. The total effect almost borders on the surrealistic. It's really about a room as sculpture, incredibly tactile and encompassing but with a revolutionary softness and sensuousness. Particularly appealing is the way the eye moves across the surfaces in exploring the interpretation of space.

It's no mere fancy that Boffrand's designs make you feel like a finer person. I believe that our surroundings should be a reflection of who we want to be as well as who we are. And a Boffrand room makes you feel like a better person. Boffrand and the other designers I have selected as my mentors are aristocratic as they address what is best and better in us in some way emotionally. It is not a moral judgment being passed; instead, the rooms bring the inhabitants and visitors to a higher realm of consciousness and intellect.

An octagonal foyer I designed for the late Sir James Goldsmith's Mexican estate, Cuismala, in 1988 owes its inspiration to that particular design by Boffrand. As the entry hall, the space had to surprise the viewer and alert his or her senses. I also wanted the eye to move through the space and study both light and shadow in an inventive manner.

Treating space emotionally may seem a lost battle since people in general are impervious to emotions. Yes, they are aware of silly sentimentalism but not attuned to true grandeur; they tend to discard it as pretentious. Those same people also mistake vulgar display of wealth for elegance. The wealth of someone's home should

PHOTO: AKG LONDON/ARCHIVES CDA/GUILLOT.

A detail of the ravishing Hôtel de Soubise by Germain Boffrand, which Robert Couturier frequently references in terms of the eighteenth-century designer's preference for treating space as sculpture. Both order and fanciful detail make Boffrand distinctive.

not be crushing but should be presented as a gift to those who visit. The eighteenth century and Boffrand seem to have understood that perfectly.

For the Goldsmith project, I borrowed from Boffrand's treatment of space in a surrealistic manner. If you study the main building, you can

PHOTO: FRANÇOIS DISCHINGER.

The foyer of the Cuixmala main house by Robert Couturier owes a debt to Germain Boffrand with its interplay of light and shade.

see that I aimed for not just creativity but a serious kind of amusement. Even the colors—a sunlit terracotta with a dash of chevron in deep navy—give an element of surprise, almost a kind of extravagant rococo palette. And there's a touch of sensuousness to the shapes.

Another lesson that I take from Boffrand is his profound belief in the ultimate effect of design. Like Boffrand, I deeply believe in the potential impact of design. Boffrand wrote in 1745, "The character of the master of a house . . . can be judged by the manner in which it is arranged, decorated or furnished." That is my goal—to create a residence that expresses the personality of the owner. At best, the design should speak neither loudly nor pretentiously.

It's the completeness often based on the highest principles laid down in eighteenth-century France—the combination of the extreme attention to detail, exacting craftsmanship, and rigorous geometry spiked by contemporary imagination—that I believe gives a heightened presence. Yes, fineness of materials and execution are critical, but the design should not be about glorifying cost. The aesthetic pursuit is paramount.

In addition to Boffrand, there are two particular architects I pay homage to and return to again and again. Both in their own way are radical pioneers in the treatment of space.

Cuban-born architect Emilio Terry (1890–1969) is best known for his highly idiosyncratic Chateau de Groussay for Charles de Beistegui. To Terry, effect was everything. He once noted, "A room without a cornice is like a man without a collar." And the library is the height of superb decorative effect. The space is tall, yet long, with books from floor to ceiling and a gallery reached by two spiraling staircases. Trompe l'oeil paintings and intricate medals cover the

A central courtyard with a trio of double-decked arches spanning each side gives a sense of order and lightness. It is the ideal outdoor room and garden in one.

walls, while marble busts of Roman emperors guard the mantelpiece.

Having sat in the library numerous times, I have often wondered how such an enormous room filled with thousands of things from books to medals to small statuettes could be so comfortable. The paintings and objects—their very textures—keep one's mind wandering with delight and discovery. And the upholstered sofas covered in simple white slipcovers make one want to stay forever.

As to Terry's treatment of beautiful things from Grand Tour obelisks to Sèvres porcelain to military medals, he never used them to create a sense of forbidding awe but rather with a mixture of reverence and a sense of fun. He never displayed antiques to impress or belittle visitors, but really to ornament life, because he believed life was better with beauty around.

His real talent was the modernity of his approach to French eighteenth-century architectural language. Unequivocally, he knew that

The living room of the Los Angeles home of Maryann O'Donnell is emblematic of Robert Couturier's use of French and American hallmarks of furniture design. Above a T. H. Robsjohn-Gibbings sofa, specifically designed for his famed Casa Encantada in nearby Bel Air, is an iconic Serge Roche mirror along with a period German globe.

language so well that he felt at total ease with it, and that is why his particular style was called Louis XIX and never Louis XVI.

Above all, Terry respected the past without slavish imitation yet with sublime inspiration. He took the essence of a vanished time and adapted it to the present. Nobody lives today the way they did in the eighteenth century, and to pretend that is a falsehood. Emilio Terry never pretended that Charles de Beistegui was the reincarnation of the Prince of Soubise. Terry treated architecture with humor and lightness. Nothing at the chateau is ponderous. And the chateau was not truly about money; Groussay was built during the war, when there was no beautiful material available.

Proof of just how fetching Terry's designs remain is the fervor for his examples. At the Paris Biennale, his furnishings, some of which are high Empire meets surrealism, sold out immediately.

To see how I applied Terry's principles by highlighting hallmarks of the decorative arts in an interior so they appear as if made for the space, simply consider the Los Angeles residence of Maryann O'Donnell. Examples by Jean Royère, Gilbert Poillerat, Jean-Michel Frank, Serge Roche, and Jacques-Emile Ruhlmann set an inherently French tone yet represent the spirit of the owner. They are the real decorative elements of the house.

The third pioneer to whom I turn frequently is Eileen Gray (1878–1976), the Irish architect, furniture designer, and lacquer artist. Remarkably precocious, she was a pioneer of the International Modern style, and her furniture of tubular steel, glass, and aluminum remains dazzling to this day.

When I was 20 and a student at the École Camondo, I was captivated by her designs and

Using pivotal objects from the decorative arts with extraordinary comfort and warmth marks Maryann O'Donnell's dining room. The sleek Jacques-Emile Ruhlmann chairs grace a rare Jacques Adnet and Maurice Louis Savin dining table.

PHOTO: MARY E. NICHOLS.

desperately wanted to own her iconic chaise lounge, which to me was the opposite of all I had ever known. And although it really contained nothing in terms of details, I found the result dazzlingly attractive. I could hardly afford the original, even though my grandmother admonished me, "You can't possibly buy something as pedestrian as a copy." But I turned to a copy, a rather good one with nickel feet. I still treasure the chair and it now graces my apartment in Paris. The line is sinuous—undulating but controlled. As a chaise, this example is not really about comfort or cozying up for a long read on a cold winter day but how good the sitter can look. You don't slouch in that chair, you recline—quite elegantly, I might add. After all, isn't comfort a middle-class invention?

Gray's furniture, whether it be a lacquered screen ingeniously louvered, or a single chair, is really about refreshingly new spatial relationships and the innovative use of materials. In her case, she used—heaven forbid—cheap materials and created designs about extreme simplification, which is the height of sophistication. I borrow her remarkably pioneering sense of independence and innovation along with her fascination with simplicity of line. Like Boffrand and Terry, Gray treats objects sculpturally.

Today, with so few having the time to reflect on anything of importance, referencing the refinement of the eighteenth century through Boffrand, Terry, and Gray is critical. Their treatment of design sculpturally remains the height of elegance.

The richly furnished Port Royal Parlor showcases du Pont's attention to color harmony and symmetry.

Elissa Cullman

~ *on* ~

HENRY FRANCIS du PONT

Each trip I make to Henry Francis du Pont's Winterthur is a pilgrimage. As I tour the extraordinary rooms, I always experience a deepening of my passion for American antiques and Americana.

I was first introduced to Winterthur in 1969 as a newlywed, before I had any interest in antiques or interior decorating. My sister-in-law brought me to Wilmington, Delaware, to see Winterthur, du Pont's great country estate museum, in order to school me in the preferred Cullman family aesthetic of Americana. This was the inner sanctum of the world's largest collection of American decorative arts: 175 lovingly decorated rooms brimming with 88,000 objects including masterpieces of painting, furniture, silver, and metalwork as well as a myriad of porcelains, pottery, and glass. This journey was the beginning of my education in the canon of all things American, and the wellspring of my later career as an interior designer.

At that time, Winterthur was not open to the public; one could only tour the estate with a private guide in a very small group. Our guide was one of the graduate students from Winterthur's distinguished masters program in early American culture. He was knowledgeable, articulate, and enthusiastic, and I was enchanted—from my first glimpse of the graceful ellipse of the Montmorenci staircase to the robust carving of the Van Pelt high chest.

Mesmerized, I explored every corner of the house. There was so much to see, but I never felt overwhelmed. Countless collections of antique furniture, fabric, and objects were all artfully, respectfully, and painstakingly arranged and displayed in rooms boasting expertly restored historic paneling and architectural details. Moreover, du Pont had not designed stale period panoramas of history. Instead, his rooms were lively and welcoming, reflecting the energy, passion, and erudition of the man who lived within them.

In the early 20th century, American decorative arts were looked upon as inferior to their European antecedents. Henry du Pont was a pioneer. Rather than being influenced by the popular taste of his time, he turned instead to the American decorative arts, taking delight in our native cultural heritage. This "awakening" occurred on his 1923 visit to the home of Electra Havemeyer Webb (who later founded her own museum) in Shelburne, Vermont, where he saw a pine dresser displaying a set of pink Staffordshire plates. Ruth Lord, du Pont's daughter, describes her father's reaction, telling us that "the novelty and beauty of the pink china against the butternut color of the wood" was a defining moment for him, almost a revelation.[1] It was this newfound appreciation for the understated elegance of the American decorative arts tradition that led in time to the creation of the Winterthur museum we know today.

What distinguished Henry du Pont from simply being a collector was his astounding ability to arrange his collections and his innate if unspoken talents as a designer. Joe Kindig, the renowned antiques dealer, once observed, "Harry du Pont is like a conductor of music. He might not know how to play each and every instrument, but he knew how to blend them together exquisitely."[2] When asked, Du Pont attributed his honed senses of proportion, color, and composition to his love of the natural world. He felt that he had unconsciously absorbed these sensibilities growing up surrounded by flowers and gardens. "I have always loved flowers and had a garden as a child . . . and if you have grown up with flowers and really seen them, you can't help [but] have unconsciously absorbed an appreciation of proportion, color, detail, and material."[3]

On every visit to Winterthur I am struck by the rhythm and beauty of the acres of gardens and the astounding vistas. I wonder if my own affinity for decorating, like du Pont's, could be traced to my interest in nature. The two years I spent in Japan studying ikebana—the classical Japanese art of flower arranging—and its principles derived from the order and harmony of the natural world made an indelible impact upon my later career as a decorator.

I feel a profound connection to Henry Francis du Pont in that he was never trained as a decorator; his decorating was rooted in collecting. I too began as a collector, spending the weekends of my young adulthood scouring the

The painted and grained woodwork of the Fraktur Room creates an exciting setting for du Pont's collection of Pennsylvania German Arts such as fraktur, pottery, and furniture.

countryside for nineteenth-century spongeware pitchers to fill the shelves of my painted setback cupboard. My love of collecting and my affinity for folk art brought me to the Museum of American Folk Art, where I curated "Small Folk: A Celebration of Childhood in America" in 1980. This exhibition and the accompanying book analyzed attitudes toward children in America as revealed through the folk art of the late seventeenth, eighteenth, and nineteenth centuries.

But I had no thought of a career in decorating until I coauthored a screenplay with my dear friend Hedi Kravis in 1984. We submitted our effort to a well-known film producer who had just won an Academy Award. While he quickly determined that we had absolutely no talent at script writing, he thought we had always shown a flair for decorating. He proceeded to hire us on the spot to decorate his Park Avenue apartment, and our career was launched.

Though we were both well educated and well traveled—two particularly important attributes for any designer—we had not gone to design school or trained at a design firm. We turned to du Pont and to his rooms and writings for guidance, employing the same classic principles of

The abstract simplicity of folk painting, seen on this well-preserved panel of woodwork, inspired modern artists of the early twentieth century to collect American folk art.

design as he did. Like du Pont, we emphasized color harmony, balance, and order. We wanted to design not just pretty rooms or period rooms, but homes filled with comfortable seating, antiques, and objects of interest and color and life.

Today, I continue to aspire to du Pont's level of creativity and ingenuity, and I strive for my rooms to be restrained but not dull, elegant but never flamboyant or opulent. Du Pont's constant attention to detail never ceases to amaze me. The minutiae of fabric and fringe obsessed him as completely as the overall decorative

scheme of every room at Winterthur. On a recent trip I was particularly taken with the dining room. I have always loved the curtains there, with their valences of inverted triangles. We've adapted this design more than once. But on this visit I realized that the triangles in the curtain headings echo the inverted triangles on the backs of the Sheraton chairs. This fluid and subtle bit of detailing gives the room an extra layer of meaning and complexity.

In appraising du Pont and his monumental contribution to American decorative arts, I am also awed by his recognition of the importance of the architectural envelope in creating a successful interior. He understood that the collections he was assembling would be more sympathetically displayed in rooms that also had historic architectural significance. As a result, he sought architectural interiors from Virginia to Vermont and installed these settings—walls, floors, and plaster ceilings included—at Winterthur. This passion for architecture has also been one of the guiding principles of our work. At Cullman & Kravis, we collaborate very closely with architects on all of our projects to ensure that the architecture is in harmony with the decorating. As we like to say, architecture comes first, and there is no successful decoration without good "bones."

One of my favorite rooms at Winterthur is the Port Royal Parlor, Henry du Pont's paean to eighteenth-century symmetry and balance. One of his first principles of design warns, "If you walk into a room and right away see something, then

In this exquisitely colorful room, du Pont used a hand-painted eighteenth-century Chinese wallpaper depicting scenes from everyday life as a backdrop for his collections of decorative arts in the Chinese taste.

you realize that that shouldn't be in the room."[4] In the Port Royal Parlor, he expressed harmony and cohesiveness not just in the colors and finishes, but also through complementary upholstery and furniture, floor coverings, walls, and windows. In this room, warm yellow silk damask unifies the symmetrical arrangement of Chippendale sofas, chairs, and curtains. Two spectacular high chests flank the room and frame the furniture within. In fact, du Pont outbid William

Randolph Hearst for the second of these, paying the highest amount ever for a piece of American furniture at that time. Although the two chests were used as counterpoint to each other, neither dominates the other elements in the room.

My living room in New York City is an homage to the Port Royal Parlor in many ways. The subtle glazing on all of the walls and woodwork is derived from du Pont's use of historic painting techniques; even the eighteenth-

English and American antiques, custom upholstery, and treasures from travels abroad warm my Park Avenue living room, inspired by the Port Royal Parlor at Winterthur.

century Adam mantle, which I found in London, is overglazed to blend with the tones I chose for the original 1929 woodwork of the Rosario Candela building. Like du Pont, we at Cullman & Kravis are forever searching with artists for the ideal glazes, stencils, and techniques to balance the tones in a room, never wanting any one thing in the room to jump out.

This room also reflects our belief that a successful interior should have an abundance of layered lighting and reflective surfaces. Du Pont loved to make his rooms shine too. He amassed significant quantities of lighting fixtures and

devices, pottery, glass, and metalware. He lit period fixtures with tiny candelabra bulbs, which was revolutionary in his time. At Cullman & Kravis, we activate our rooms similarly—using old and new silver, polished and dull brass, glass and cut crystal, reflective mirrors, gilded frames, and a variety of warm woods and finishes to make every room glow and sparkle.

One of the functions of my living room is to showcase various collections such as the Chinese export figures on the mantel and Kangxi vases mounted as lamps. A home should reflect the owners' lives and be able to evolve with

PHOTO: ALEC MARSHALL.

Inspired by the Fraktur Room at Winterthur, the woodwork in my family room in the country is glazed and hand stenciled. Whimsical (and colorful) American folk art fills the room, while comfortable custom upholstery adds to the relaxed mood.

them. Every tabletop and surface is enriched by my collections of treasures and the stories they tell of my hobbies, interests, and travels. But though the room is filled with precious objects, it is well used and enjoyed. We love to gather here as a family and to entertain our friends.

While Winterthur is perhaps best known for its formal American furniture and objects, for me it was and will always be the folk art collections that I love most. The bold carving of the Schimmel eagles, the stenciled painting on the Mahantongo chests, and the abstract swirls of intense color on the spatterware pottery seem

so modern and fresh. In fact, along with du Pont, the first collectors of American folk art were the modern artists of the early twentieth century—Sheeler, Demuth, and Kuniyoshi. They of course were followed by pop artists Warhol and Lichtenstein. This folk aesthetic is the style that has been most closely associated with my decorating work.

One room in particular at Winterthur has been influential in our decorating. Du Pont had an entire eighteenth-century room from the Hottenstein House (1734–1890) moved to Winterthur. Called the Fraktur Room, it is known for the collection of eighteenth- and nineteenth-century German records of marriages, births, and baptisms (fraktur) that hang on the paneled and folk-painted walls. Du Pont recognized this remarkably inventive and quirky paneling as a uniquely American idiom. Though worn with time and age, the paneling in the Fraktur Room continues to project its original richness, elaboration, and beautiful abstraction.

The whimsical spirit of the Fraktur Room inspired the design for the woodwork for my family room in our country home. I thought about what a folk artist would have done had he or she been given the room in 1950, and the

Detail of the glazing on the woodwork, country living room.

result is reflected in the no less than seven painting techniques—from fingerpainting to dragging to combing—that define the doors and moldings. Each line of woodwork was separately taped and painted. Even the crown molding was faux marbled in a folk spirit. The artist could have painted anatomically correct marble, but he got it just a bit wrong in homage to his predecessors. The vibrant palette and exuberant painting techniques are lovingly indebted to the Fraktur Room.

The Chinese Parlor at Winterthur is an extraordinary example of the degree to which du Pont loved to layer the pieces in every room, visually and intellectually coordinating the objects and furniture with each other, with the wall coverings, and with the overall color harmony of the room. In his Chinese Parlor, the Chinese scenic wallpaper is a backdrop for his American furniture in the rococo and Chinese taste. The room is exquisitely colorful—a lovely shade of antique green silk damask on the curtains and slipcovers beautifully complements the paper, ceramics, and silver.

The inspiration for my dining room in New York City is the Chinese Parlor. When I walked into that room in 1969, it was the first time I was enveloped 360 degrees by scenic wallpaper. In the 1980s, my husband and I bought our first "grown-up" apartment, and I immediately called Gracie, New York about the paper—did they have anything like it? Indeed, they had 40 linear feet of a very similar paper dating from the mid-eighteenth-century Qianlong Empire. They created the additional 36 feet needed to completely wrap the dining room in the panorama. Of course, I commissioned the extra footage because it was too important not to go all the way, as in the Chinese Parlor at Winterthur.

The dining room reveals three of my passions: American antiques, seen in the Hepplewhite sideboard and chairs; chinoiserie, as evidenced by the eighteenth-century wallpaper, nineteenth-century carpet and porcelains; and oenophilia, demonstrated by the collection of nineteenth-century decanters and the grapevine border in the Chinese rug. There are so many layers in this room.

As my career as a decorator progresses, I am called upon to design homes for a variety of clients in a broad range of styles, not just American. Although I cannot always work in the Winterthur aesthetic I love so, and I could never be the purist that Henry du Pont was, he has been and will always continue to be my mentor. As an interior decorator for collectors of fine art and antiques, I recognize and validate du Pont's insight that while collecting is at the core of designing, collections must not dictate lifeless museum rooms; rather, they should enhance, enrich, and enliven the atmosphere of our homes. Whenever I begin work on a new project, I feel as if Henry Francis du Pont is looking over my shoulder, bolstering my conviction that a successfully decorated room should strike a balance between historical accuracy and aes-

PHOTO: DURSTON SAYLOR.

Clearly influenced by the Chinese Parlor at Winterthur, the highlight of my dining room in New York City is the antique Chinese wallpaper, which completely envelopes the room.

thetics while also responding to the functional demands of modern life.

[1] Ruth Lord, *Henry F. du Pont and Winterthur, A Daughter's Portrait.* New Haven, CT: Yale, University Press, 1999.

[2] As quoted in Jay E. Cantor, *Winterthur: The Foremost Museum of American Furniture and Decorative Arts.* New York: Harry N. Abrams, 1985.

[3] Denise Magnani, *Discover the Winterthur Garden.* Winterthur, DE: The Henry Francis du Pont Winterthur Museum, 1998.

[4] *Oral History with Harlan Phillips,* April 11, 1962.

John Dickinson's living room in his transformed firehouse, San Francisco. After years of paint were peeled off, the grand salon walls and ceiling were glazed. The chairs are nineteenth century; the rest of the furniture is Dickinson's designs, which have become classics and an inspiration to many designers. The animal leg–inspired collection of tables is truly a Dickinson hallmark. The accessories were selected on the basis of their natural beauty rather than luxury or pedigree.

Orlando Diaz-Azcuy

~ on ~

JOHN DICKINSON

I first met San Francisco interior designer John Dickinson in San Francisco in 1976 when we were both invited to participate in the planning and founding of a new design school. The legendary decorator, admired for the clarity and intelligence of his interiors, had made his mark on the American design scene with a series of white plaster tables and boldly sculptural furniture designs, as well as the neutral palette of his decor. He was at the height of his career. At our meetings, I was impressed by his lack of pretension, his good humor, the generosity of his ideas and participation, and his fastidious professionalism.

Many design insiders consider John Dickinson the most original, innovative, and influential American interior and furniture designer. He died in 1982 at the age of 62. Dickinson polished his design for four decades, perfecting decor that was as elegant and apparently effortless as a Fred Astaire dance routine—and as enjoyable to witness.

John Dickinson's signature style is unmistakable. His interiors and finishes are like those of no other designer. At a time when California design was typified by overscaled sofas and chairs, unrelenting beige, chunky stone tables, and pine beds, Dickinson's rooms were subtle, timeless, roman-

Display at Macy's Department Store for the introduction of Dickinson's new line of furniture in 1978. In his attraction to nature, Dickinson went as far as to imitate the natural animal body structure and sometimes the human body. The incorporation of bone images is clearly expressed in this table and lamp. The seating is upholstered in canvas to give a casual look and at the same time the skirt to the floor provides elegance.

tic, and somewhat austere. His references were esoteric and arcane—early Egypt, thirties Paris, the late Regency, Stonehenge, prehistoric Egypt, obscure Parisian craftsmen.

A grand and theatrical four-poster bed John designed for an artist friend in 1967 is a virtuoso construction of steel piping with brass trim. Dickinson dressed the bed in yards of camel hair and gray wool suiting fabrics, and covered bedroom walls with black and white herringbone tweed.

Dickinson did not rely on a riot of color for his effects. His room schemes were done in colors like smoky topaz or palest pink or shades of white. White painted pine tables, galvanized tin tables, and white plaster lamps of his own design were often used in dramatic counterpoint to a custom-crafted chrome fireplace, natural canvas-upholstered sofas, taupe leather-cushioned chairs, and flat gray industrial carpet. In my own work, too, I prefer beautifully executed interior architecture and understated color. I'm Cuban, so I do love a splash of color or a dash of gold as counterpoint.

Always in evidence in Dickinson's work were flashes of wit (tables with animal feet, "airport art" displayed as if it were priceless sculpture), a reverence for historically important designs of the past, and simple, almost unobtrusive lamps and tables in sculptural shapes.

I admired Dickinson's great discipline in furniture placement and arrangement, his lack of flash, and the truly great sense of luxury and comfort even in quite modest rooms. Open any design magazine today, or visit any show house where the work of up-and-coming designers is on view, and Dickinson's singular influence is apparent. John Dickinson's rooms had no pre-

A display exhibit from 1978, when John Dickinson's furniture designs were introduced at Macy's department store in San Francisco. Notice the simple architectural expression of the chairs as well as the storage cabinet along the wall. The human plastic figures add an element of whimsy to this dramatic display.

tensions, no frills, and no faddish style, and today more than ever I see young (and experienced) designers turn to him for that discipline.

Soon after I first met him, John Dickinson designed a highly original (and controversial) 25-piece furniture collection for Macy's interior design department in San Francisco. Soon afterward, he would complete the original super-chic

decor for the Sonoma Mission Inn, and was in demand among the Pacific Heights mansions for his extravagantly imagined interiors.

The dashing and debonair Dickinson would be seen around town in his sleek vintage black Jaguar, its flanks laminated with natural woven cane in homage to early Parisian carriages. He would appear at design events in his Gap chino pants and Huntsman tailored jackets (often

PHOTO: JOHN M. HALL

The living room of the Diaz-Azcuy residence in New York City overlooking the East River. The apartment is a very Zen expression, reflective of the comfort of quietness and light. It is finished with a limestone floor and the wall is painted in a matching color. The apartment houses a collection of early twentieth-century furniture and painting with a Dufour paper wall panel. The carpets are part of the collection of very old Samarkand rugs. The painting is by Christian Bérard, the stool is by Robsjohn-Gibbings, the tub chairs are English Art Deco, and the sofa bed and coffee table were designed by ODA.

worn, offhandedly, with sneakers) and leave early. He had no interest in being lionized.

Like Jean-Michel Frank, John Dickinson was fanatical about details, finishes, edges, and the smallest refinements. Nothing about Dickinson's rooms was left to chance, but they never looked stiff, intimidating, pretentious, or showy. Chairs were to be used and moved about a room; pillows were to be leaned on. Lights were for illuminating reading or drawing; tables were the right height for books, glasses, or magazines.

Dickinson, who grew up in Berkeley, was opinionated, witty, erudite, generous, thoughtful in his comments, and always down-to-earth. He understood the design paradox Andree Putman calls "rich and poor"—expensive upholstery details worked in plain canvas, an elegant slipper chair upholstered in white Naugahyde, or plain muslin curtains done in the most Balenciaga way with lavish detailing. John Dickinson's rooms were not based on ephemeral effects or momentary trends. "I don't put my stamp on a room by styling, doing things like plumping cushions a certain way or fluffing up the curtains. Then design becomes so ephemeral. Basic construction of a room should be where good design comes from, otherwise it is not really style," he commented.

Still, for all his opinions, this was clearly a man with a sense of humor. "Taste is a word I avoid," he noted. "Good or bad, it's all so nebulous. The more you're dealing with taste, the

PHOTO: JOHN M. HALL.

Window detail of the Diaz-Azcuy residence in New York City. This window overlooks the East River. The black marble console is a disguise for the heating unit and serves as a display surface for Diaz-Azcuy's accessories collection. The egg is a Japanese store sign, as well as the wood beads. The hanging display shelf is from Japonesque, a store in San Francisco, with a Jean Dunand brass vase on it. The stool is 1930s French in wrought iron and leather. The bed has a luxury white damask bedspread from Nobilis.

more you're on shaky ground. Vulgarity to me is another matter. Vulgarity has great vitality." White plaster lamps, mirror frames, and coat hangers for the I. Magnin couture department sprouted like twigs; a console for a Telegraph Hill apartment had the rough texture of adzed stone;

PHOTO: MATTHEW MILLMAN

The elegance and grandeur of this living room are expressed by the presence of two chaise lounges in indigo blue and gilded design by Orlando Diaz-Azcuy Designs and provides at the same time a casual seating to a grand salon for entertainment. The carpet is by Orlando Diaz-Azcuy for V'Soske Design collection. Over the newly replaced Brazilian blue marble mantle is a painting by William DeKooning. The table in white lacquer is by Orlando Diaz-Azcuy Designs.

and a three-legged lamp base was inspired by an African tribal stool. One stylish custom-made (expensive) table for a Presidio Heights mansion looked, Dickinson said, "like rough boards pegged together by a five-year-old."

The white plaster tables with animal feet Dickinson designed in the seventies are now highly in demand in the auction/antiques dealer vortex of New York, Los Angeles, and Paris. "I would say that the Regency or Egyptian influence was not in my mind when I first designed chairs and tables with animal feet," Dickinson told me. "I was after something mock primitive and quite surprising. The fetish-y thing is quite marvelous and it hadn't been explored at all. Designers usually have gone the other way, taking primitive design and refining it way beyond recognition. That way you usually end up with something banal. If you go the other way, as I did, you usually end up with something very peculiar looking but quite successful."

Dickinson's rooms for carefully selected clients were done in muted colors or shades of white, although he did splash out for one daring client and use five shades of green with a dash of palest pink. White plaster tables, galvanized tin tables, and white plaster lamps of his own design were often used in dramatic counterpoint to natural canvas-upholstered sofas, taupe leather-cushioned chairs and a serviceable gray carpet.

"People think I never use color, but it isn't true," he commented. "Their eye just isn't trained, and they don't notice subtlety. Subdued colors are still colors. But really, the reason I can't use strong color with conviction is that it draws attention away from all the things I do best which involve line, proportion, and shape. Anyway, a color scheme is a questionable device on which to base a room design."

In evidence were flashes of wit—a cluster of simple Kenyan carved tables, lacquered white and displayed as if they were sculpture, reined

with formal sofas or an Art Nouveau table. "You cannot do a lasting room design based on a current fad or novelty," Dickinson said. "There's a fine line between being amusing and being eccentric. A whole room based on whimsical things would not be a laugh."

John set the highest demands and standards for himself and for the teams of craftspeople who executed his work. He was always paring his designs down, never adding, never romancing a room with frills or what he called "fluff." This is a discipline I follow myself, in every commission. "Prettiness has nothing to do with style," John told me. "Logic precludes prettiness. If you're stripping down rooms, as I do, there's no place for it."

Like Jean-Michel Frank, John Dickinson was a perfectionist. Nothing about his rooms was left to chance, and he often described himself as a draftsman first, a decorator second. Still, his rooms never looked stiff, pretentious, or labored. Chairs were to be used and moved; pillows were to be leaned on. Lights were for reading or drawing; tables were the right height for books, drinks, or newspapers.

Accessories that made walk-on appearances in his San Francisco Victorian firehouse residence over the years (and that turn up with surprising frequency in rooms by Dickinson's designer admirers) include baskets of white conch shells, white ceramic phrenologist heads, white bowls of onyx eggs, large stoneware bowls of bleached bones, brass fire hose nozzles, plain

white ironware ashtrays and dishes, hand-carved African stools and headrests, branches of white coral in white ironstone cachepots, and gray river stones or crystal eggs in white bowls. While some of these objects are now selected by in-the-know designers, Dickinson pioneered these collections at a time when pretentious gilded objects and vermeil trifles were in vogue.

John Dickinson understood that lasting designs should not be over-the-top or theatrical, but rather understated. "There are many places in a house that do not warrant expensive furnishings," he observed. "It's really not essential to spend everywhere. Muslin curtains can be the prettiest things in the world if they're sewn beautifully. You just don't have to make a big production of everything in a room."

Still, for all his severe pronouncements, Dickinson had a sense of humor. "I take what I do very seriously but I don't like designs to be too serious," he told me. "You know, this can be a very formal profession. I just like to have a little fun with the work I do."

OPPOSITE: *View of Orlando Diaz-Azcuy's dining room in his residence in San Francisco. A contrast statement to a 1936 traditional Spanish home with beautiful ceiling brackets from a fifteenth-century Spanish convent (originally owned by William Randolph Hearst), and the Saarinen white marble dining table, an Ellsworth Kelly lithograph, and a Japanese ceramic sculpture on the table. And finally, complimenting the decor, Neapolitan eighteenth-century gilded chairs and a chandelier designed by ODA for Boyd Lighting as part of the Opera collection.*

PHOTO: DAVID DUNCAN LIVINGSTON.

Boudin's masterful use of saturated color to create interior drama is nowhere more clear than in the front hall of Windsor House in Paris.

Jamie Drake

~ *on* ~

STÉPHANE BOUDIN

Master and Man

What was it Cocteau said? Something like, "Don't confuse seriousness with gravity." That's how I feel about my work. And that's also how I think Stéphane Boudin may have felt about his. The distinction is an important one, especially if you're interested in discovering what makes the decor of a specific room or house simultaneously fabulous and livable—both right for the place and as a stage for the person occupying it—and differentiates it from that of another banal, or overbearing, or just plain silly interior. It's hard to pin it down, because quality is difficult to describe, and, when it comes to interiors, often elusive. But, like art (or pornography), you know it when you see it.

Most good decorators share a passion for detail, an eye trained to evaluate scale and proportion and craftsmanship, and a better than average knowledge of the history of interiors and the decorative arts. Great decorators, however, transcend the past—some by refusing to recreate it, others by reinventing its ideals in the terms of their own times. Stéphane Boudin was definitely one of the best when it came to placing the past perfectly in the present. He, and his colleagues at Maison Jansen, translated that very French, rather lofty belle idée of the grand interior—the extremely specific, Gallic, eighteenth-century style with its boiseries, gilding, saturated colors, sumptuous fabrics, and

The architecture of a room always dictated the style of its interior. French Empire proved to be the logical choice for the White House's Red Room, a predominantly neoclassical space with a mix of architectural elements, some original to the house and some from later restorations. The McKim, Mead & White 1902 alteration moved the French Empire mantel into the room and installed the Monroe-era door and window frames and twentieth-century cornice, chair rail, and wainscoting as complements.

glorious furniture—into rooms that not only suited their occupants' ambitions and personalities, but also celebrated the finer things in life in ways that were completely appropriate for the twentieth century.

Boudin was to the mantel born, so to speak, in 1888. His father, Alexandre, designed and made passementeries. Boudin, who studied at the College de Juilly, later joined the family firm. He was 35 when he joined Maison Jansen in

*The dining room of Windsor House illustrates Boudin's ability to translate the French idea of the grand interior—
the specific Gallic eighteenth-century style—into a space that not only suits its occupants' ambitions and personalities but also celebrates the finer things in life in ways completely appropriate for the twentieth century.*

1923, after showing the family's latest trimmings to Henri Jansen. By then, the House of Jansen had left behind its rather humble beginnings as a small furniture shop, opened on the rue Royale in 1880, and evolved into the complete source for everything having to do with interiors after completing the restoration of the Lacken Royal Palace in Belgium and making significant splashes in St. Petersburg at the 1899 Franco-Russian exhibition and in Paris at the 1900 Paris Universal Exposition. Jansen not only had a complete workshop filled with the works of master artisans skilled in all the trades of furniture manufacture and metalwork, but also an encyclopedic collection of reference works on period textiles and furnishings, as well as pattern books.

In decoration, as in other fields, a little knowledge is a dangerous thing. There's nothing more important than connoisseurship when it comes to the decorative arts. In order to educate the client about history and quality, you need to understand completely, for yourself, what they are. The education never stops, and should never stop, because you can never know it all. The more you see, and the more you look, the more you sharpen your critical eye and your ability to judge. If you want to create a room or a residence filled with delight, you must comprehend the various traditions of the different artisans whose skills can utterly transform a commonplace space into a place of wonder. The respect for fine craftsmanship, the obsession with the details of a room, the finishing of a window treatment, the accessorizing of a sofa— these are just good beginnings.

Boudin was a master teacher. He had cultivated himself and was brilliant at educating those of his clients who were interested about the arts of the interior—which in turn helped Jansen continue to flourish. His knowledge of period styles and the techniques of traditional craftsmanship impelled Maison Jansen to its exalted position as the firm of choice during the middle of the twentieth century. In addition, Boudin supervised the firm's acquisition of eighteenth-century paneled rooms, which he later installed in numerous houses around the world.

Boudin had the reputation of a man without pretensions. He was known for his wit, his wonderful sense of humor, and his beautiful manners (Paul Manno, his longtime associate in New York, once said that Boudin always interviewed his clients himself, and made a point of not working with anyone "who could not laugh"). More to the point, Boudin was renowned for his encyclopedic knowledge of the history of French decorative arts and interior design; his connoisseur's eye; his matchless understanding of scale and proportion; and his innate, unique, and bold color sense.

Boudin's capabilities as a colorist are among the skills of his that I find most intriguing and instructive—largely because I love strong color and interiors with a lot of movement. His signature palette was aqua, orange, and rust. Mine

PHOTO: WILLIAM WALDRON

Like the White House, Gracie Mansion has been altered many times over the years. In renovating the mansion's ceremonial rooms, such as the parlor shown here, I wanted to balance the need for historical accuracy with the desire for the most appropriate style of furnishings and decor. They're not always the same thing. Finding the best solutions for these kinds of rooms requires a certain flexibility and a definite but well-informed vision—as Boudin's work at the White House demonstrates.

PHOTO: FRITZ VON DER SCHULENBURG.

Boudin's use of saturated color and signature furniture pieces in Windsor House clearly influenced my work on the interiors of this London townhouse. The mix of modern art with antiques creates a certain element of interior theater.

tends to the chromatic scale of the fauves, with orange, aqua, yellow, and purple. He habitually designed elaborate window dressings, sometimes running continuous valances around the entire room, almost always using lambrequins, voluptuous draperies, and, of course, tassels and other forms of trimming. He also used paint like a magician, creating enormously grand, rather stagy wall finishes—not quite classical trompe

l'oeil, with its architectural bias, but definitely backgrounds with a theatrical bent.

We know Boudin, of course, as Mrs. Kennedy's ultimate secret decorating weapon and arbiter of taste during the celebrated early 1960s restoration of the White House interiors—a difficult role he filled in an extremely gracious fashion. Working on historic properties, especially when they belong to "the people" rather than the client, is never easy—as I've discovered for myself with the renovation of Gracie Mansion, the official residence of the mayor of the City of New York, which was concluded in 2002. These jobs require the best of your decorating abilities, as well as the utmost of your historical knowledge. They also tax your diplomatic skills in unusual ways—normally, there's a committee overseeing the process, partly for cost and partly for historical accuracy. In Boudin's case, at the White House, Henry Francis du Pont and John Sweeney of Winterthur regularly weighed in with the strict curatorial points of view. Sister Parish also put in her two cents, and so on.

Many of the Boudin and Maison Jansen interiors are long gone, and many were never photographed. Fortunately, Boudin's three spectacular residences for the Duke and Duchess of Windsor were clearly appropriate for the occupants, the architecture, and the site. His client list also included the King of Belgium, Mrs. Winston (C. Z.) Guest, Nancy Lancaster, the Paleys, the Charles Wrightsmans, the Shah and Empress of Iran, Elsie de Wolfe, and Lady Olive Baillie, whose Leeds Castle he helped restore and redecorate. The photographs that do exist reveal interiors that demand strict adherence to the disciplines of proper etiquette and dress code—no casual Fridays here, please! This, the photographs say, is a designer who, in creating environments of unsurpassed formal beauty, ensured that his

PHOTO: FRITZ VON DER SCHULENBURG.

In the dining room of the London townhouse, I've brought together elements from the same period but from different traditions—English, Irish, American, and French Empire. Boudin's attention to scale and detail, and the comfort he had with layering pattern upon pattern, informed my choices here.

clients strove to live up to them and up to the best of themselves—without, one hopes, ever letting the effort show. You never get the sense that Boudin repeats himself. He uses the tools of his trade elegantly, with infinite variety, and with gusto and enormous good humor. So forget gravity, and get serious.

Arthur Dunnam

~ *on* ~

JED JOHNSON

All of us who endeavor in visually creative fields are in a constant state of absorbing and assimilating the stimuli that intrigue and excite us: details, colors, objects, proportions, placement, techniques, textures, this bit of pattern, that elegant mosaic, the line of a chair, perhaps the cut of a garment, the layout of a spectacular garden, an incredible painting or piece of sculpture. From an early age we are drawn uncontrollably to these things. As the years pass, we begin to realize that by assimilating, sifting, and sorting all of these bits and pieces of visual stimuli we form a sense of our own personal vision of beauty, of correctness.

The learning process never seems to cease, and as a result of this continuum we are always honing and refining our view of perfection. As I reflect on the path I have taken in forming my own sense of self as a designer thus far, I feel incredibly fortunate to have been associated with several individuals whose intelligence, sensitivity, and personal styles were instrumental in allowing me to make enormous leaps in my knowledge of the real world of design and most importantly in formulating a strong and definite sense of my own vision as an interior designer.

My first part-time job as a design assistant was in the office of Arthur Smith. Arthur, a fellow southerner, had been the business partner of

Billy Baldwin and upon Mr. Baldwin's retirement had continued the business as Arthur E. Smith Incorporated. Many of Mr. Baldwin's celebrated clients remained with Arthur, and during my six years there I had the unparalleled experience of working on a number of projects for Harding and Mary Wells Lawrence. Their legendary residences were absolute perfection, and they opened my eyes to a world that I had previously explored only in books and magazines. Being exposed to these functioning residences that combined palatial architecture; magnificent settings; and clean, comfortable, and sexy interiors that managed to evoke the locale of each residence in an elegant and entirely chic way established an entirely new standard for me to strive for.

In November 1986, longing to find a work environment that would allow me to take on a broader range of design responsibilities, I began my career with Jed Johnson and Associates as a project designer and began to learn the true meaning of perfection. Although I had known Jed Johnson socially for several years, and was aware of the mystique of his Warhol affiliation, we were not really very well acquainted at that point. Like many people in those days, I was

PREVIOUS SPREAD: *A fusion of eighteenth-century elegance and twentieth-century comfort, this St. Louis living room with its soothing subtle colorations, incredible quality, and attention to detail epitomizes a Jed Johnson traditional interior.*

under the misconception that Jed's work was all about Arts and Crafts. While I appreciate Gustav Stickley's furniture and feel that it has its place in certain interiors of today, it is by no means the pinnacle of interior design for me personally. This incorrect assumption regarding Jed's work was my only hesitation in accepting a position with his firm. Luckily, when I came to the interview, Jed showed me portfolios of his work and I realized that this was exactly what I wanted: a firm that was not tied to any signature style but explored a whole range of periods and approaches rooted in traditional interiors—the formality, elegance, and restraint of eighteenth-century rooms; the exuberant and richly patterned layering of late nineteenth-century English and American interiors; the swank and sexiness of Jacques-Emile Ruhlmann and Jean-Michel Frank; the picturesque whimsy of Hispano-Mooresque villas by the sea filled with tile work, dark robust seventeenth-century furnishings, and ironwork; masculine and comfortable mahogany-paneled suites outfitted with gutsy William IV furnishings that would have been completely at home in an English gentleman's club, and Louis, Louis, Louis. All of this and more was the work of Jed Johnson.

Jed Johnson was by nature a quiet and reserved man. He would never command a conversation by being the loudest or most obvious participant. It was his immense restraint that gave such power to those words he did share. I watched many times as men and women accus-

PHOTO: © JOHN M. HALL.

Superb English Georgian furnishings are complemented by a palette that is unexpectedly rich in its own restrained way—a crisp, edited mood that feels almost modern in this Fifth Avenue sitting room by Jed Johnson.

tomed to taking charge and being in complete control amended their opinions after listening intently to a few whispered sentences from Jed. They knew that if he made the effort to voice an opposing view, it was something he felt strongly about; and if they had been working with him over an extended period, they had also come to realize that he was almost always right. Jed was

never destined to be a public speaker; I think the thought of it absolutely petrified him. This may have contributed to the lag time that elapsed in Jed's name being familiar to a larger public: he was simply not one to call attention to himself. Here he was designing residences for Yves St. Laurent, Peter and Sandy Brant, and Mick Jagger and Jerry Hall, not to mention

A seriously elegant room designed to be lived in. French furnishings from the eighteenth through the twentieth centuries combine with sofa side tables designed by Johnson and a commanding Ziegler Sultanabad carpet from Simon Franses to create a perfect harmony that defies categorization.

Andy Warhol, and no one beyond a small and rarified circle was yet aware of his name. This was soon to change in 1991 with the publication of an article titled "The Education of Jed Johnson" in *House & Garden.*

I mention Jed's reserved, gentle, and generous demeanor because it is impossible to separate those qualities from his work. A Jed Johnson interior was never flashy or cacopho-

nic, but always spoke quietly and was composed of the absolute highest quality: furniture, fabrics, carpets, art, and especially craftsmanship. Jed put worlds of wonderful detail in his rooms, but they revealed themselves, like Jed, softly, over time, not bombarding all at once and fighting for attention.

As we worked together, I soon became aware that all of these varied and beautifully detailed interiors were the result of an immense amount of research and an equal amount of—for lack of a better word—anguish. Jed was not one of those designers who walk into a room and commence "creating" as if it were performance art. If the job involved an existing structure, and the structure had merit, Jed would spend untold hours poring through his library and extensive cache of clippings looking for a historically appropriate basis. If the project happened to be a new residence, he would consider the location, the climate, and what style might best compliment all the givens, and then off to his library he would go. It was all about creating something based on historical precedent, yet slightly unexpected and fashioned uniquely for a particular client's particular residence.

Often a very special antique carpet or monumental piece of furniture would be the genesis of a room. For Jed, it wasn't simply about finding something that was nice enough to do the job. He had a formidable ability to impart his passion for and knowledge of a truly special thing to a client. Jed encouraged his clients to pursue a quality level that they hadn't been aware of before meeting him, but which they appreciated and absolutely required after time spent in his tutelage.

There were always folders of fabulous items from all over the world in Jed's office: Sultan-abad, Agra, and Aubusson carpets, carved stone chimneypieces, chandeliers of every description, antique marble mosaics that might become a

PHOTO: © ERIC BOMAN.

Swedish neoclassical furnishings combined with the whimsy of Rene Prou's gilt metal chairs strike a relaxed and inviting tone amidst the grandeur of elaborate mid-nineteenth-century architecture in this East Coast sea captain's parlor designed by Arthur Dunnam.

coffee or dining table, rooms of eighteenth-century Chinese wallpaper or nineteenth-century tooled and polychromed leather, and incredible mirrors that were like works of art, to name only a fraction. He would gather these images in his travels or they would be sent by dealers who knew his taste and would be methodically filed away until he could find just the right home for them. With each new commission, he would pore over photos to see which of his store of treasures might be perfect this time.

This same fastidiousness and insistence on quality and appropriateness permeated every aspect of a job. Once an aesthetic direction was chosen and a few key elements locked into place, Jed would immerse himself in every aspect of a project. He believed that to have a truly great room you had to start with great "bones." For such a seemingly delicate and soft-spoken man, Jed didn't mind softly saying to the client that a gut renovation was absolutely necessary, that nothing less would achieve the perfect end result: "Just because it's old doesn't mean it's right!" In renovations, he liked making things as great as they should have been in the first place. Because of all of his painstaking research, the end result often seemed so appropriate and in sync with the existing architecture that the viewer would assume it had always been there. I remember one total interior gut renovation of an 1898 Stanford White oceanfront cottage on Long Island that involved removing roomfuls of 1950s knotty pine paneling and sliding glass doors to be replaced by elegant and intricately detailed McKim, Mead & White–inspired detailing. Jed received the supreme compliment of an octogenarian who remarked on seeing the fin-

ished product, "It's exactly as I remember it when I was last here, as a boy."

These flawless results were due not only to great design, but also to an insistence on superlative craftsmanship. Jed was a magnet for artistically minded craftsmen. He worked with an array of artisans who could (and still can) flawlessly execute any design that could be dreamed up. Carvers, sculptors, glass workers, ironmongers, custom tile makers, goldsmiths, gilders, decorative painters, wood finishers, weavers, embroiderers, cabinetmakers, tinsmiths, rug hookers, eglomise specialists, plasterers, and stonemasons are only a fraction of the specialty workers needed to execute and realize a Jed Johnson–designed residence. The gentle coaxing and appreciative praise that was always forthcoming from Jed drew from these artists their best efforts. Jed made me acutely aware that the unique talents of those who execute our work must always be respected. A good designer must often be a buffer of calm between the demands of an overly optimistic schedule, a flurry of trades on the job site, and the craftspeople who are all eager to do their best.

Jed was inspired by an array of designers and architects, both past and present, and brought aspects of their work to his own. William Morris and the English Arts and Crafts movement were particularly close to his heart. The textiles, carpets, and patterns that Morris employed in his work were a continual fascination for Jed. The unusual color combinations and seductive tex-

Strictly serene, this Long Island waterfront living room designed by Arthur1 Dunnam is an elegant homage to the handmade. From the hand-hooked rug by Stephen T. Anderson to the custom-embroidered sofa fabric by Chelsea Editions and the beadwork center table topped with a Dale Chihuly sculpture, every piece is a delight for the eye.

tures found in these crewels, embroideries, appliques, and hand-knotted concoctions often found their way into Jed's rooms. Jed not only gave me an appreciation for Morris, but he also opened my eyes to the beauty of lighting by W.A.S. Benson, the glazed pottery of Christopher Dresser, and the work of so many others on our shopping trips to England.

Of equal interest to Jed was English architecture and design of the eighteenth century.

PHOTO: © JOHN M. HALL

The twentieth-century sensibility of this living room overlooking Manhattan's Central Park is achieved with a carefully edited selection of furnishings that spans the eighteenth, nineteenth, and twentieth centuries. An important eglomise table by Pierre Legrain for Elsie de Wolfe, as well as Jacques-Emile Ruhlmann's low table of macassar ebony, ivory, and shagreen, anchor the room designed by Arthur Dunnam.

The proportions of Robert Adam's neoclassical designs, which he introduced me to at Syon House and Osterley Park; the exquisitely carved furniture of Thomas Chippendale (particularly chairs) that we were always on the lookout for in our many shopping expeditions; or William Kent's masterful creations and the voluptuous damasks, taffetas, and Axminster carpets to compliment them all appealed immensely to Jed and there were many examples of these to be found in his files at any given time. Volumes depicting the designs of Stéphane Boudin and

Jansen were also to be found among Jed's well-thumbed library. He greatly admired Boudin's ability to create something historically correct, yet modern, in its comfort and most importantly in its restraint. Employing the finest elements and having the end result be immensely inviting, not intimidating, was a constant theme in Jed's work and in the creations of those he admired.

Of his contemporaries, Jacques Grange and David Mlinaric were perhaps his favorites. Grange's unexpected combinations of art, furnishing by twentieth-century masters, and picturesque finds from the nineteenth century, as found in the residences of Yves Saint Laurent, were in Jed's opinion masterful. Mlinaric's extensive work for the National Trust Properties in England was, for Jed, thrilling to behold as it combined superlative interior furnishings with the most exquisite architecture imaginable.

As Jed's reputation grew, he continued to be the same modest, soft-spoken gentleman. He taught by example and always seemed to find a tactful way to suggest that a better solution might be found. All it took was a little more diligence. I believe his work was not only stimulating for him, but also a source of immense fun. Jed always managed to find some aspect of fun and humor in even the most ordinary of tasks; I will always remember the many laughs we shared. Jed's accomplishments, abilities, and vast knowledge of so many styles, periods, and movements are all the more impressive considering that he was entirely self-taught. Working with him was an incredible learning experience for me. No titled professor has had nearly the impact on my design education as this quiet and thoughtful man who, in addition to being a designer well worthy of inclusion in this book, was also a friend whose warmth and generosity of spirit are missed by so many.

Ronald A. Grimaldi

~ *on* ~

ROSE CUMMING

I was fortunate to have been raised surrounded by considerable beauty as a child, as both of my parents had a great love for beautiful houses and furniture, and I happily ingested every detail of the redecoration of various rooms. At age 12 I was allowed to choose the colors and some furniture for my bedroom and bathroom. It came off quite well, and I have been addicted ever since.

However, my first foray into the business world was in advertising at J. Walter Thompson, which did not turn out well on either front. My next job was at Tiffany & Company, in a management position that added a dimension to my knowledge of china, silver, and so on. But it was not until a serendipitous turn of events occurred that I ended up working with Rose Cumming, whose office at the time was in a beautiful and majestic old building on Park Avenue and 59th Street. I have been here ever since.

Rose Cumming arrived in New York during the Great War of 1914 from her native Australia en route to England where she was to be married. This, however, never came to pass as there were no passages on transatlantic sailings for nonmilitary personnel. Lunching one day with an old New Yorker, Frank Crowninshield—who, at the time, was editor of *Vanity Fair*—she complained of utter boredom just flitting around

New York being social. Mr. Crowninshield suggested that perhaps she should get a job, to which she replied, "I am perfectly useless. I do not know how to do anything!" Mr. Crowninshield suggested that perhaps she would like to become a decorator, to which she answered, "Perhaps I would, but first tell me what it is!"

Decorating as we know it today was in its infancy, with Elsie de Wolfe just beginning to make her mark in that field. Before that time, a woman would call in an upholsterer and select materials of her own choice. But as for a decorator, no one had ever heard of such an animal.

"Crownie" introduced Cumming to Mary Buel, a rather famous decorator in New York at that time, and she found herself with a job. Almost immediately, she knew that this was to be her greatest love. She never married.

Miss Cumming, as she was invariably called, wrote the following in 1929, and it is still applicable today: "Interior decorating is the frivolous sister of the architectural profession. It requires primarily that one be an expert in color, design, period and the placing of furniture. Most of us have added some knowledge of architecture to our equipment as decorators, so that being con-

versant with the laws of proportion, line and so forth, we can intelligently interpret the original design of the architect. A decorator should, in addition be blessed with a sixth sense—a kind of artistic alchemy which endows the articles of furniture with that elusive quality of livableness which transforms houses into homes. No amount of training or schooling can teach you this. Either you have flair or you haven't."

When I arrived at the shop, Rose Cumming's sister, Eileen Cumming Cecil, was the doyenne; she was an absolutely spectacular woman with whom I became very close. A few years passed, and on more than one occasion, Mrs. Cecil would comment that this or that thing that I did or said sounded exactly as if Rose had said it. Coincidence, we thought, until one day I mentioned that my birthday was approaching and a friend had invited me to join him in Stockholm. When Mrs. Cecil asked me when that was, and I told her, she whacked her forehead with the palm of her hand, almost toppling the extravagant hat she wore, and exclaimed, "My god! That's Rose's birthday! No wonder you're so similar!"

Rose Cumming's loves were passionate and legion. Never restricted to a particular period or style, she assembled a room as a great chef would combine ingredients. Her sister, Eileen, summed things up rather succinctly. She said, "Rose, there are only three things you really love: you love everything to look frightfully

PREVIOUS SPREAD: *"In real decorating, there are no precedents," said Rose Cumming. Here, in a 1935 dressing room in the Ambassador Hotel, New York City, a mirrored screen and silver-leafed walls depict her unconventional style.*

Rose Cumming's eccentric and theatrical living room in her New York City townhouse, circa 1937, with eighteenth-century hand-painted Chinese wallpaper, Louis XV furniture, and an eighteenth-century Venetian chinoiserie chandelier.

fresh, frightfully clean, and frightfully well cared for." But Miss Cumming also loved old mirrors, glittering chandeliers, and highly polished floors, where the old wood and the furniture always looked their best.

Her sense of color was unique: the daring mix of chartreuse with Persian blue, cloth-of-silver hangings paired with violet satin, and the unusual combination at the time of chintz and silks existing happily together in tow. Hereto-

PHOTO: ROSE CUMMING COMPANY.

Rose Cumming's glamorous and almost surreal style is reflected in her bedroom with silver lamé draperies, silver-blue foil on the walls, and an exotic East Indian daybed.

fore, chintz had been relegated to country rooms and thought far too rustic for city houses. Today, this, of course, is a cliché. Her sense of place was factual. If a comfortable chair was needed for reading, she plopped one in. If a light was needed in a certain corner, a lamp of suitable scale and beauty would find its rightful place. In summation, Rose Cumming's credo was that she liked houses or rooms that present a potpourri of many styles and periods—a harmonious, romantic, lush, and beautiful mixture of everything.

For her, decorating was a trial and error thing, like trying on hats until you find one that fits your face.

First came the room; next, the collection of suitable furnishings, which she would place in the middle of the room. She then would begin pulling and dragging everything back and forth, trying objects here and there until she found the exact place in the room where this or that piece looked the best, and there it stayed—almost forever.

Above all, she believed in good "bones." Of all the graceful features that a room should possess—a fireplace, proper placement of windows, polished parquet floors, and so on—the most important of all was a high ceiling. "It makes every woman look beautiful when she enters the room; but if a low ceiling practically scalps her, she comes into the room looking like a pigmy."

I must admit that I find it extremely easy to carry on the feel and style of Rose Cumming as I have the same belief that there are no rules in

Kips Bay Decorator Showcase, New York City. Painted Louis XVI twin beds with a half tester draped in silk in the master bedroom; 1930s Venetian chandelier and a 1940s mirrored console; Regency bench; chinoiserie wooden wall cabinets; 1930s beaded peacock lamp.

PHOTO: PETER VITALE.

Ronald A. Grimaldi New York City entrance gallery—antique Chinese mirrored screen; Chinese Regency export sofa covered in pale green satin; Louis XV chandelier of crystal and bronze; eighteenth-century Chinese silk embroidered wall hanging.

decorating. An inspiration occurs when I begin a new job that is coupled with practicality and common sense. Appropriate furniture for the room and a client's lifestyle then come into play. Of course, backgrounds are extremely important and should be given top priority. A beautifully painted, glazed, or lacquered room with well-polished floors can stand on its own merit and with the addition of curtains and a chandelier can be very satisfying to the eye, even before all the furniture and trimmings arrive.

I do believe that creating a good room depends on one's ability to impart a feeling of ease and comfort and a sense of permanence so that the room has an evolved look rather than a "look at me, I've just been decorated" feel. Of all the creative qualities a decorator possesses, having an eye—that elusive thing that can create magic—is by far the most important.

Rose Cumming began her illustrious career in 1917 and continued until her death in 1968. She left behind a very special legacy and one that I am very proud to have inherited.

Palm Beach living room with a French carved walnut roundabout covered in zebra silk; nineteenth-century Italian gilt wood open armchair upholstered in leopard silk; Louis XVI gilt wood barometer.

PHOTO: CARLOS DOMENECH.

David Hicks's living room, named "the long room," at Britwell, 1970; a symphony of clashing reds and pinks in the green Oxfordshire countryside. Pink felt stuck to the walls, paintings made to his specifications, Louis XV chairs in purple tweed, a pink sandstone horse head bought from the carver in Agra, on a stainless steel base.

Ashley and Allegra Hicks

~ *on* ~

DAVID HICKS

Text by Ashley Hicks

When I was a child, my father would spend hours drawing bizarre illustrations of the growth of his "Design Empire" and attach them to the long, excitable letters that he sent me at whichever grim boarding school I was then attending. The most vivid of these, which now hangs in our country kitchen, shows a tree growing from what he labeled "rich Essex soil" (Essex being the county of his birth). From its branches hang rolls of David Hicks carpet, wallpaper, and fabric; the shop signs of his various outlets across Europe; his series of *David Hicks on . . .* books (on decoration, on bathrooms, on living with taste, etc.); and a small architect's set square

with my own initials, ALDH. As he constantly reminded me, I was named Ashley Louis David Hicks in order that one day, when I succeeded him in our nascent design dynasty, I could drop the first two names and bear his with pride.

As I am my father's only son (my sisters, in his determinedly Victorian view, should certainly never work for a living), he saw me as the crown prince of decorating and himself, naturally, as the king. Like any princeling, I was coached in the ways of kingship, and so taken to every museum, monument, or interesting house that he could find, which I loved. July would find us in the South of France, examining every detail of the neo-Grecque Villa Kerylos at

PHOTO: ESTATE OF DAVID HICKS.

David Hicks's bathroom at Britwell, 1965. As children we would say good morning to him every day as he lay in the tub. A 1730 paneled room, the bath clad in paneling to match, all stippled paint faux granite. The loo is hidden by the brass-nailed black screen. The geometric carpet is his first design adapted from mosaic tiles in Isfahan.

Beaulieu or the modernist Fondation Maeght; August, in Ireland, escaping the humdrum routine of our summer holiday by touring the vast Palladian mansions of the decaying Irish aristocracy or staying with Henry McIlhenny at Glenveagh; September, on a client's yacht—without the client—drifting around the Aegean, drawing Doric temples and Crusader castles.

At Easter, we would be in the Bahamas, in the austere, cement-walled modern house my father had modeled on the ancient Egyptian tomb of King Zoser at Saqqara. On the way, we would stop in Miami at another client's house and visit Vizcaya; on the island, he and I would go round the enchanting local villages of pretty colonial wooden houses painted clear, bright pastel colours, sketching (and occasionally stealing, as decorative accessories to be mounted on the wall) their fretwork brackets and balusters. Christmas was always spent at Broadlands, my Mountbatten grandfather's home, where my father would point out to me every nuance of the neoclassical interior. In between, apart from occasional visits to London, I would be at school, kept abreast of the progress of the David Hicks empire by letter.

When my wife Allegra and I began to design interiors together, we went through a process of assimilation, coming as we did from very different upbringings. She had grown up in a completely modernist environment in Turin, Italy, her parents banishing anything more than 10 years old from their home, a glass house designed by her father and furnished sparsely with only the best new Italian and Scandinavian design. This was quite unlike my own home, Britwell, a grand eighteenth-century country house in Oxfordshire, England, where my father mixed old and new with a hand so sure that nothing ever looked out of place. We had both received academic trainings in design of different kinds; after four

David Hicks's drawing room at Britwell, 1965, showing walls hung with oatmeal woven cotton and a table of his design with Python skin top. The design shows his use of a very neutral color scheme of off-white and biscuit with accents of color through his elaborate "tablescapes," (here yellow and blue) and his mix of old and new with abstract paintings and classical sculpture.

Allegra and Ashley Hicks's living room in the country, 2001, with walls painted to imitate stitched-together squares of green leather, which my father said was the one good thing we ever did—"You know, I really rather like this room . . ." The overscaled cornice and the symmetry show his influence; the "muddy" colors do not. On the floor, an Allegra Hicks rug. Cabinets to the left and right of the fireplace, with inset panels of Punjabi embroidery, hold the television and stereo.

years of art school, I had trained as an architect at London's Architectural Association; Allegra had studied graphic design in Milan, painting at the École van der Kelen in Brussels, and decorative art history at Sotheby's in London.

At first, I was burdened with the conflicting dogma of my modernist schooling and my aesthetic upbringing; Allegra with the rigidity of her modernist upbringing. She succeeded in ridding me of my father's irrational loathing of the forties and fifties, while I introduced her to the joys of traditional pattern and classicism. Gradually we adapted to each other's way of seeing and found our own path and vocabulary. I began as an architect, designing interiors and the occasional exterior, concentrating more and more on the details until I began to design my own collection of furniture, while Allegra moved from painting rooms in trompe l'oeil to painted furniture and then pattern making, which led her to rugs and fabrics and, more recently, fashion.

My father's work has influenced us in many ways. He mixed old and new—placing modern abstract paintings with antique furniture of every period and exotica like Indian statuary; using a modern stainless steel base for a classical sculpture beneath eighteenth-century pictures; covering fine antique furniture with a modern geometric printed fabric; using the silhouette of a 1650s Swedish curtain pelmet in crisp white linen in a minimalist white room. He looted the past to make the modern, doing it so skillfully that most of his rooms look completely undated and timeless 40 years later. Allegra and I revel in absorbing influences from every historical period and drawing on these in designing new pieces, but blending the sources until there is no one obvious root.

While studying at the Architectural Association—known for its radical modernism—I spent hours dwelling on eighteenth-century Parisian house plans, obsessing about classical planning, which I had first discovered with my father. He had learned what he knew of archi-

PHOTO: ASHLEY AND ALLEGRA HICKS.

Allegra and Ashley Hicks's dining room/studio in the country, 2001, built as a tribute to my father's memory after his death—he loved octagonal rooms. On the outside it has "rustic" columns—in fact, tree trunks from our woods, with bark intact. At left and right are bookcases he designed. He would have hated the 1950s Italian table and chairs and Allegra's "Flame" sofa at left. Curtains in Allegra Hicks "Tree of Life" cotton.

tecture from books, from visiting houses, and from looking at monuments, but had naturally a powerful, instinctive feeling for those qualities of proportion and symmetry that create harmony, and passed on some of this to his little prince. Just as he raided Swedish palace bedrooms for

Allegra and Ashley Hicks's London dining room. The color scheme was derived from the curtains, woven in 1937 by Marion Dorn for my grandmother Edwina Mountbatten's Park Lane penthouse. The walls were painted by Allegra with billowing "curtains" of Turkish cintamani design. I scraped the paint off the original 1850 plaster cornice, an early David Hicks idea. Ebonized dining chairs are Ashley Hicks's "Thar" design. My father did not like the room's earthy terra cotta pink colors at all.

pelmet designs and scoured Owen Jones's *Grammar of Ornament* for ancient Chinese geometric patterns that would make good modern carpets, so he looked back to history for the most basic design rules. All of this training has stood me in good stead and often I have marveled at how the

application of symmetry and good proportion can utterly transform an interior.

Other influences that Allegra and I have drawn from my father are in color and lighting. His use of color was often slightly overpowering in its strength, but never inharmonious. A room entirely in clashing reds, pinks, and purples (and he made many of them) sounds like a nightmare, but in his master colorist's hands even this palette produced an effect of great beauty. He would saturate a room with one main color, using subtle variations and only the very occasional detail from a different part of the spectrum—the whole framed, usually, by white-painted ceiling, moldings, and chair frames that grounded and lightened the interior. While our own use of color is very much less strident and dramatic, we do follow his rules. In lighting, too, we follow his guide that a room should have as many varied sources of light as possible, but that you should never see a light bulb. This simple rule is tremendously effective.

While Allegra and I, consciously or unconsciously, follow these rules of his, we approach the making of rooms from such a different angle from my father that his influence is in fact limited. My father always had a dread of appearing indecisive or confused; he saw the world in black and white—or rather, in shocking pink and white. He was brought up by his mother to show total conviction at all times, to be ready with an instant and sure response to any question. I remember my housemaster at school asking him what color to paint the new sports changing room. He replied with his habitual certainty and to the housemaster's obvious dismay, "Purple." One of my father's favorite recipes for an interior was yet another update of an historically successful technique, where he would divide walls into well-proportioned panels with bands of paint, paper, or upholsterer's braid. He loved to frame, to compartment, to clearly define edges; it gave a sharply tailored, organized look of instant elegance and enabled him to impose good proportions on bad.

My father's inspiration was always fame, glamor, excitement; to make a big noise, a lasting impression. Strong visual impact was his aim, making a definite and original statement, often at the expense of comfort. He had, in fact, checked himself out of the hospital while dying because of its overabundance of plastic and the nurses' unappealing apparel. He also liked the idea of rooms whose perfection slightly intimidated visitors, and even clients, as though under a magic spell that might be broken if anything was moved. Allegra and I start, instead, from a more user-friendly perspective, aiming to produce a more relaxed and easy environment, where the obvious signs of life that enter any inhabited room—the newspapers, magazines, children's toys, the visual chaos of everyday life—need to be accommodated, and no room should be destroyed visually by them. In color, we may follow my father's rules, but not his incandescent schemes of vermilion and scarlet, which can be a little threatening for ordinary mortals. We use subtle variations of

Allegra and Ashley Hicks's London living room. Walls are painted a sandy beige within a strong white architectural framework—very much my father. All the furniture is an Ashley Hicks design. From left: "Klismos" chair (adapted from 430 B.C. Athenian original) "Adam & Eve" tables, "Bronze-X" ottoman, and "Drum" table. The early Georgian mirror hung over my father's fireplace in his house on the next street in 1965. The rug is Allegra's "Spheres," which my father would have hated since it is not geometric.

what he called "muddy" colours, which can give great beauty but also visual comfort and ease. His yearning for absolute definition and certainty is not ours; we enjoy the ambivalence of uncertainty, of hints, suggestions, and touches, rather than his hyperbolic fireworks.

The fireplace is the most important architectural element of a room, from which the design of the rest of the room takes its cues, including its decoration. Edith Wharton's own dining room at 884 Park Avenue in New York illustrates this.

Thomas Jayne

~ on ~

EDITH WHARTON
AND OGDEN CODMAN'S
THE DECORATION OF HOUSES

I have a great admiration for Edith Wharton. I'm captivated by her fiction, especially *The House of Mirth* and *The Age of Innocence*. Both novels are enriched by the author's descriptions of architecture and interior decoration; they further her narratives and form a finely textured, accurate, and firsthand view of the Gilded Age. They delight the mind's eye of the aesthete.

As a decorator, though, I most admire her lesser-known first book, *The Decoration of Houses*. In contrast to her fiction, this treatise on interior decoration, written with the architect Ogden Codman, deftly dismantles the late Victorian taste she knew so well and argues for the revival of a purer, more classical tradition.

Wharton and Codman especially favored the grander period now considered to be the first modern decoration. In *The Decoration of Houses* they catalog an extended history of architecture and design—a first in books on domestic interiors. And, most important, they manage to distill and illustrate their taste for general readers in a practical, very specific way.

Because of this firm grounding and populist bent, much of what they wrote a century ago is applicable to my work. I particularly appreciate their primary thesis: that the design of houses ought to be based on beautiful proportion with simple "unconfused lines." They skillfully argue for the importance of finding the qualities of suit-

A graceful French lit de repose and an elegantly designed desk in The Mount's library prove that well-chosen furniture should complement the architecture and proportions of a room.

COURTESY OF BEINECKE RARE BOOK AND MANUSCRIPT LIBRARY, YALE UNIVERSITY.

The use of tapestries, lamps, and statuary—or "bric-a-brac"—if well placed and selected—need not make a room feel cluttered or distract from its good form. Another view of the The Mount's library shows how to integrate these elements into a room's decor.

COURTESY OF BEINECKE RARE BOOK AND MANUSCRIPT LIBRARY, YALE UNIVERSITY.

Wharton and Codman thought that dining tables with center supports were practical, but could stand improvement in their design. As noted in The Decoration of Houses, *dining chairs should have wide, comfortable seats and be low so they do not interfere with service.*

ability, moderation, fitness, and relevance, which "give permanence to the work of the great architects." One of their better-known passages summarizes their refined point of view: "Proportion is the good breeding of architecture. It is something, indefinable to the unprofessional eye, which gives repose and distinction to a room in its effects as intangible as that all-pervading essence which the ancients called the soul." To my eternal amusement, they added a simpler but equally resonant statement: the decoration of houses is not "a branch of dressmaking."

One remarkable and useful aspect of the book is that Wharton and Codman's ideals of

good design are arrayed, illustrated, and defended in 16 "how-to" chapters written in charming Whartonian prose. They begin with "The Historical Tradition" and "Rooms in General," then proceed to "Walls," "Doors," and so on, followed by room types, from "Entrances and Vestibules" to "School Rooms and Nurseries," and finally ending with a discourse on "Bric-a-Brac."

Most of the references to architecture and decoration are of the grandest sort, including, for instance, a view of the Library of Louis XVI at the Palace of Versailles or the Antechamber in the Villa Cambiaso in Genoa. But the parallel understanding of and advocacy for simplicity is

Wharton and Codman noted that pictures representing life and action often grow tiresome when looked at over and over again, day after day. Walls decorated with fruit and flowers might be predictable, but are not without decorative purpose.

to Wharton and Codman's everlasting credit, and of great value to any decorator working today. When discussing economy, they wrote: "When a room is to be furnished at the smallest possible cost, it must be remembered that the comfort of its occupants depends more on the nature of the furniture than of the wall-decorations or carpet. In a living-room of this kind it is best to tint the walls and put a cheerful drugget on the floor, keeping as much money as possible for the purchase of comfortable chairs and sofas and substantial tables. If little can be spent in buying furniture, willow arm-chairs with denim cushions and solid tables with stained legs will be more satisfactory than the parlor suit turned out in thousands." In essence, this is a description of today's simply painted rooms and the equivalent use of wicker and sisal, a combination my firm employs widely.

Still, it is the vivid descriptions of the formal rooms more typical of a century ago that speak to me. I love the fact that that they are featured in the text because rooms of this nature are so rare now. The authors argue that the "Gala" rooms meant for general entertainments—ballrooms, salons, music rooms—should never be used for "any assemblage small or informal enough to be confidently accommodated in the ordinary living room." To fulfill this purpose they must be large, "very high studded," lit by chandeliers, and not overcrowded with furniture. In this age of the multipurpose "Great Room," these rules are, of course, difficult for us to follow. The notion of rooms being so specific and discrete in their purpose is clearly out of favor. But, in truth, who would not prefer a separate comfortable living room as well as—if circumstance allowed—a ballroom used only for big parties and other special occasions? This makes more sense than one very large space filled with the modern equivalents of overstuffed parlor suites. What's the point of all that space if it doesn't enrich one's life? Wharton and Codman's discussions of formal rooms are fascinating to me in the way that

PHOTO: SCOTT FRANCES.

A comfortable living room by Thomas Jayne in a New York townhouse. As Wharton suggests, every effort has been made to capture the light of the three front windows to give the room a sense of comfort.

old-fashioned etiquette books are: obviously, times have changed and people behave differently now, but those books can impart a certain philosophical frame of reference that causes me to ponder and assess my own understanding of suitability, relevance, and appropriateness.

A singular opportunity to work in Edith Wharton's taste came with the chance to decorate a room at her house, The Mount, in Lenox, Massachusetts. I was asked to decorate the den—a corner room on the piano nobile—of her husband, Teddy Wharton. The original contents of the room were lost, and the room was never photographed in Wharton's time. So I was asked to decorate it as if Wharton were alive today, using *The Decoration of Houses* and my knowledge of their personalities for inspiration.

Teddy Wharton, a sportsman and bon vivant, ran the estate and collected wine. The marriage, plagued by his depression, was troubled. According to my firm's brief, he needed a comfortable room of his own that was part office, part bolt hole. "Beauty depends on fitness, and the practical requirements of life are the ultimate test of fitness," *The Decoration of Houses* announces. This became our primary text in creating his den.

We retained the room's original boiserie designed by Codman. Rather than picking out the paneling in two colors, as is the popular taste, I chose to paint the walls one color—a

Teddy Wharton's den, as envisioned by Thomas Jayne. The Mount, Lenox, Massachusetts. The philosophy of comfort in a man's den is reflected in the use of comfortable chairs (favored by Wharton and Codman) and the introduction of drink tables. They noted that too often there was a "lack of those simple comforts which [men] find at their clubs."

light tobacco—in response to the Wharton-Codman dictum that the fewer colors used in a room, the more pleasing and restful the results will be. They also wrote: "In well-finished rooms the order is usually imagined as resting, not on the floor, but on pedestals, or rather on a continuous pedestal. This continuous pedestal or 'dado' as it is usually called, is represented by a plinth surmounted by moldings."

My "base," the skirting board, is painted gray to better enforce the idea of a pedestal. The gray, in turn, relates to the marble used for the fireplace, which centers the room, matching the classical ideal. "The fireplace must be the focus of every rational scheme arrangement. Nothing is so dreary, so hopeless to deal with, as a room in which the fireplace occupies a narrow space between two doors, so that it is impossible to sit about the hearth." Around the fireplace are arranged an upholstered sofa and chair, a modernized version of the Edwardian leather sofas that Wharton and Codman recommended for use in studies. We introduced small tables for drinks and books, omitted in Wharton's decoration but expected today. The furniture is generous in scale to provide comfort, and inviting enough to encourage a relaxed level of socializing. Wharton and Codman remarked that all too often "houses are deserted by the men of the family for lack of those simple comforts which they find at their clubs." We followed their good advice.

We used some reproduction French chairs in the Louis XV style that were favored by Wharton and appear in early photographs of other rooms in the house. Encouraged by the attention to light in *The Decoration of Houses*, the desk is practically situated by a window. There are no curtains at the windows, as a direct riposte to the Victorian draperies and "stuff hangings" so disparaged by Wharton and Codman. Instead, there are simple roller shades, decorated with a painted Italian damask pattern.

The Ford Plantation, outside Savannah, Georgia, as designed by Thomas Jayne. The economy of the sea grass mat contrasts with the French bamboo bed and the silk walls painted by Lucretia Moroni. The curtains are consistent with Edith Wharton's philosophy that they should be as simple as possible. The peacock blue chair is a triumph of Edwardian upholstery that, however, departs from Edith Wharton's own taste for simpler eighteenth-century-style upholstery.

Rather than the recommended bureau plat, which, unless of great quality, now appears predictable and dated, we substituted a modern architect's table. The carpet is a traditional Aubusson woven to my design, a version of the nineteenth-century carpet Wharton would have known. The art is a recent collage by Robert Clepper that reflects on the nature of marriage and contrasts with a pair of grisaille panels original to the room.

In the end, the result is a comfortable room, thoughtfully arranged and handsomely appointed. It is a room that Wharton and Codman would have approved of. As they said, "Originality lies not in discarding the necessary laws of thought, but using them to express new intellectual conceptions." And even though I do not consider our work at The Mount to be an intellectual triumph, necessarily, the decoration in Teddy Wharton's den demonstrates how Edith Wharton, Ogden Codman, and their book, *The Decoration of Houses,* continue to be a valuable, vibrant source of inspiration today.

Living room at Casa Amesti, Frances Elkins's house in Monterey, California. This room juxtaposes furniture of various styles and countries, but the use of the color, scale, and proportion keeps the room in harmony.

Pauline C. Metcalf

～ *on* ～

FRANCES ELKINS

"It is always fascinating to trace the influence of any important artist or designer and to consider not only why he (or she) fits into his own time, and his ideas strike a chord, but also to notice how others pick up, imitate and develop those ideas."[1] Although these words were written in reference to the decorator John Fowler, they could easily be applied to Frances Elkins (1888–1953). Her work has been revered by design cognoscenti for years. While Billy Baldwin called her "the most exciting decorator we ever had,"[2] Mark Hampton credits the quality of her influence on successors as making Frances Elkins "one of the most interesting and most significant figures in the history of American design."[3] Although many of her interiors were done in collaboration with her brother, the Beaux-Arts trained architect David Adler, for his elegant country houses in the suburbs of Chicago, others were carried out in the Bay Area of San Francisco, California, where Elkins was based for much of her life. Her talents notwithstanding, Frances Elkins's education in architecture and the decorative arts was totally guided by her brother; as her tutor, he trained her eye to comprehend all aspects of design.

Tracing the myriad sources for her taste—a broad range of architects, decorators, and craftsmen from the eighteenth to the twentieth cen-

Francis Elkins's dressing room at the Mrs. Kersey Coats Reed House, Lake Forest, Illinois. Architect: David Adler.

turies—has been an inspiration for my work, especially in the understanding of the complexity involved in putting a design scheme together. When researching Elkins's work, I learned that the most telling record of her sources was to be found in her leather-bound photograph albums; these contain images of rooms and furniture—both historic and contemporary—clipped from magazines such as *Vogue, House & Garden,* and *Country Life.* The American interiors, which range widely in period and style, include rooms from Mount Vernon and Monticello as well as the supper room in the Governor's Palace of Colonial Williamsburg with its Chinese wallpaper. They also include rooms of antiquarians/collectors, such as those of Henry Davis Sleeper at Beauport, and the much photographed twentieth-century room of Carlos de Beistegui in Paris with Le Corbusier's spiral staircase and Victorian-style silver gilt settees. The albums also contain photographs of furniture models, lighting fixtures, and decorative details designed by Elkins and David Adler as well as others designed by Jean-Michel Frank, Diego Giacometti, and Syrie Maugham. While Frances Elkins quotes from many periods and styles in her interiors, she is able to weave them seamlessly into a timeless environ. A prime example of this can be seen in her living room at Casa Amesti, her 1830s adobe house in Monterey, California, where she lived from 1924 until her death.[4] During the 35 years Elkins lived in the house, she continued to add antique and modern pieces to the rooms, but the balance and symmetry of the arrangement, so key to her style, were never disturbed. Although there are pairs everywhere in the room, they are not always used together. The juxtaposition of colors and styles, such as Chinese rugs mixed with English antiques and contemporary items, gives the room a subtle balance between tradition and innovation.

Elkins also carefully relates the color blue to the Chinese carpets, porcelains, chair covers, and even picture frames. As described by one reporter, her decoration "walks the edge between perfectly proportioned good taste (which could be dull) and bold new forms and colors (which could be excessive) . . . Elkins was a master of balance without boredom."[5] The late

PHOTO: NYHOLM/*HOUSE & GARDEN* © CONDE NAST PUBLICATIONS INC.

This bedroom decorated by Frances Elkins had walls, curtains, and quilted upholstery in the same pattern.

Stanley Barrows, the eminence grise of design history at Parsons School of Design, heralded the subtle quality of her work, commenting that "she never allowed a single theme to overwhelm her composition."[6]

Years ago I was first introduced to the work of this extraordinary decorator in a lecture given by Stanley Barrows at the Cooper-Hewitt Museum.

Dining room in New York City by Pauline Metcalf. The traditional English furnishings and collection of delft are highlighted against the dark green walls and silvered ceiling.

PHOTO: © HUGO TILLMAN.

Instantly her style struck a chord with me. Although I did not grow up in an Elkins interior, I recognized a number of similarities to the surroundings I had grown up with—a country house

OPPOSITE: *This living room, as designed by Pauline Metcalf and created from a stable, is furnished with mix of period and contemporary furniture. The use of wood, stone, and iron lends a contemporary Arts and Crafts feeling to the space.* PHOTO: © AARON USHER.

built in 1931 and designed by a Rhode Island architect, George Howe. Its architectural style, which defies categorization beyond that of Colonial revival combined with modern details, is not unlike many country places built in the 1930s by firms such as Delano and Aldrich, Harrie T. Lindeberg, or David Adler. In my own decorating experience, especially working on renovations and restorations of interiors done in the early decades of the twentieth century, I have learned

PHOTO: AARON USHER

Dressing room as designed by Pauline Metcalf in a Rhode Island house, c. 1930: built-in dressing table with large Steuben fish lights, mirrored doors, and star-shaped inlaid linoleum floor.

much from trying to maintain the look and style of this family house. From replacing fabrics to replicating curtain treatments or upholstery—sometimes tufted or seamed with fringe—it is careful observation of the details of the original style of the decoration that enables one to create a period ambience. Originally the interior decora-

tion of this country house was done by the firm of Thedlow, Inc., an early New York decorating firm located in a townhouse on East 55th Street next door to a notable competitor, the decorating firm of McMillan.[7] Like those of Frances Elkins, Thedlow's interiors were known for their style of understated chic. As such, details of Art Deco glamor could be found in the master suite dressing room with features such as a star-shaped inlaid linoleum floor and large Steuben glass fishes used as lights on the built-in mirrored dressing table. A favorite childhood retreat was the magical realm created by enclosing oneself within three mirrored closet doors.

As Elkins did at Casa Amesti, other rooms were furnished with a combination of eighteenth- and twentieth-century furnishings: the dining room has eighteenth-century French scenic wallpaper as well as a Louis XV marble mantelpiece, two runner carpets woven in Nova Scotia by itinerant craftsmen, and Sheraton dining chairs covered in off-white leather. A 1930s feeling is given to the room by four mirrored sconces and decorative glass objects including Steuben candlesticks and other pieces.

Recently, a guest room has been redecorated with a green-and-cream toile de jouy pattern for walls, curtains, and dressing table. In addition to traditional French toiles patterns such as those Frances Elkins used in several rooms at Casa Amesti, she created a similar effect in the bedroom she decorated for Mrs. Evelyn Marshall Field in Syosset, New York, in 1931. Using

Dining room designed by Pauline Metcalf at a Rhode Island house. Eighteenth-century furnishings and French scenic wallpaper and marble mantel are contrasted with details from the 1930s to give this room its period style of decoration.

printed cotton fabrics whose designs were taken from eighteenth-century copper plates became popular in America with the revival of classical taste and design initiated by decorators such as Ogden Codman and Elsie de Wolfe.

Two examples of my work in which Frances Elkins's taste and style can be seen are a dining room in New York City and a renovated conversion of a stable in southern New England. In the New York dining room, dark green walls and a silver-papered ceiling contrast with a Chinese carpet, all of which are combined with the client's inherited eighteenth-century English dining table and chairs, along with a collection of delft.

In regard to the renovation of the stable, an explanation for this eclectic space is that the client had always wanted to have a "big room"—one that would incorporate aspects of informality in a rural setting, used both as living room and dining room, but would also respect its origins as a stable. The central space was created out of two floors: the ground area, which had been used for stalls, with the hayloft above.

The creation of a large stone chimney provided the focus around which the main seating area is grouped. The original openings for the stall windows and doors were untouched; only a clerestory window was added to the upper story. The curved iron stairs and surrounding balcony are an important element in the composition of the space. The entire room is covered with boards of western red cedar, lightly pickled,

A guest bedroom by Pauline Metcalf with everything decorated in a green and cream toile de jouy print from Brunschwig & Fils.

which is a reference of sorts to the natural wood paneled rooms found often in country houses of the 1920s and 1930s as well as the original wooden siding of the stable. With Elkins's living room at Casa Amesti in mind, I combined a variety of traditional and nontraditional elements, using materials such as wood, stone, and iron to lend an Arts and Crafts overtone to the decoration. The room is furnished with an eclectic mix of styles. Initially working with the client's inherited pieces from Italy and other period sources, I combined a further mix of contemporary, antique, and 1930s pieces. A local craftsman made the iron stairs and railing as well as the two chandeliers whose foliate design is inspired by a palmetto leaf. In addition, he made two large bronze étagères for either side of the fireplace. The design for these pieces was inspired by ones that Billy Baldwin created for Cole Porter's famous apartment in the Waldorf.

The use of one color as a theme is another Elkins concept that is used to help unify the disparate mix of styles and objects in this space; in this case a soft blue-green color for the door and window trim, the floor tiles, and the painted pilasters. As with her living room at Casa Amesti, a sophisticated ambience is given to the room by the juxtaposition of such objects as two large Chinese urns, a coromandel screen on the balcony, and the original hay fork.

To absorb all the nuances of Frances Elkins's timeless style can take a lifetime, but I have no doubt that she would agree with the advice of Billy Baldwin: "No matter how taste may change, the basics of good decorating remain the same: We're talking about someplace people live in, surrounded by things they like and that make them comfortable. It's as simple as that."[8]

[1]John Cornforth, *The Inspiration of the Past* (Viking, 1955).

[2]Dupree Warrick Reed, "A New American Style," *Connoisseur* 214 (January 1984), pp. 86–93.

[3]Mark Hampton, *Legendary Decorators of the Twentieth Century* (New York: Doubleday, 1992).

[4]Since 2001, Casa Amesti has been owned by a private foundation with preservation easements to the National Trust, specifically for the main rooms. The house is open to the public by special arrangement.

[5]Reed (note 2), p. 90.

[6]Ibid., p. 86.

[7]Thedlow, Inc. (1919–1969) was among the first decorating firms to open its doors. The name of the firm was derived by combining parts of the first names of the three founding partners, the sisters Theresa and Charlotte Chalmers and Edna de Frise. The archives of the firm are at the RISD Museum.

[8]Billy Baldwin, "The Importance of Rooms People Live In," *20th Century Decorating, Architecture and Gardens* (New York: Holt, Rinehart and Winston, 1980).

Juan Pablo Molyneux

~ on ~

JACQUES-ANGE GABRIEL

Ah, influence: that always slippery topic. Who inspires you, who guides you, who prompts you, who challenges you to grow and to stretch and to think? Who is your model? Who is it you yearn to be, or to vanquish? What is your secret trick? People are always trying to turn the creative impulse into a parlor game, as though it can be spelled out in a few sentences, a few pithy points.

After working for almost 30 years as a designer, I am here to tell you that it cannot.

And here's why: influence does not begin or stop at one single moment, with one single designer or architect or artist. After you've put in a lifetime of looking, you recognize that you are part of a continuum that goes back, probably, to the cave painters and before. From very early on in human development, people have wanted to create beauty wherever they have lived, and whenever you set about making beauty, you inevitably enter into a conversation with all the people who have come before you and done some version of what you do. It is a conversation that, ideally, never stops, for as long as you live and look and work.

Naturally, of course, there are some voices that, during this ongoing conversation, speak to you a little bit more clearly—and more personally—than others. For me, one such voice belongs to the French architect and designer

The façade of the Ministère de la Marine, Place de la Concorde, Paris; known today as the Hôtel de la Marine or (in English) the Admiralty.

Jacques-Ange Gabriel . . . though, to be honest, I might as easily name his actual father, Jacques V, who was also an architect and designer, or one of his figurative fathers, like Jules Hardouin-Mansart or Andrea Palladio. But why stop there? Why not go back to the

PREVIOUS SPREAD: *The Louis XVI Library at Versailles.*

Romans? The Greeks? It is all part of the same continuum to me.

I am partial to Gabriel because, like many men of his age (the Enlightenment), he refused to be narrowly defined. He was an architect, an interior designer, an urban planner, a maker of landscapes. He moved earth; he built from scratch; he designed brilliantly on a large scale, and he worked with equal confidence on an inti-

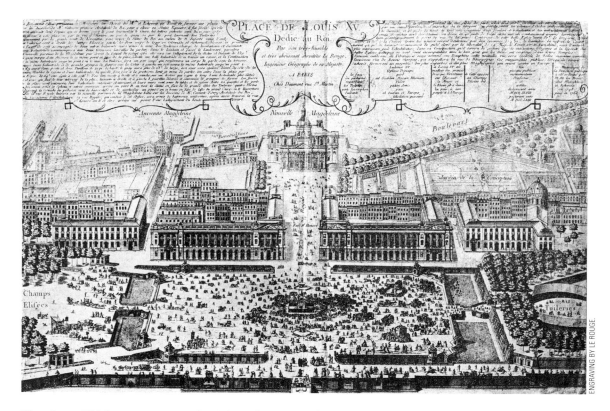

Place Louis XV, Paris, as it was in the eighteenth century. The configuration of the square that inspired Molyneux.

mate one. He was not above remodeling or redecorating his own or other people's work. He almost always brought a natural elegance to his forms, whether they were as focused as the staircase at the École Militaire or as sweeping as the Place Louis XV, now the Place de la Concorde, his great open square in Paris.

Jacques-Ange Gabriel was born in 1698 into a family where there were five generations of architects before him. Although he had his toe in the seventeenth century, he was very much a man of the *dixhuitième,* the eighteenth-century French Enlightenment. He lived a long time—until 1782—and saw many of his major works carried out when he was an old man. A favorite of Louis XV and Madame de Pompadour, he eventually held important positions in the royal hierarchy, such as *premier architecte du roi,* and he worked on many important royal and civic projects, among them additions to Versailles, enlargements to Fontainebleu and the Louvre, and the exquisite, perfectly proportioned Petit Trianon, which I am not alone in considering one of the great small buildings of all time.

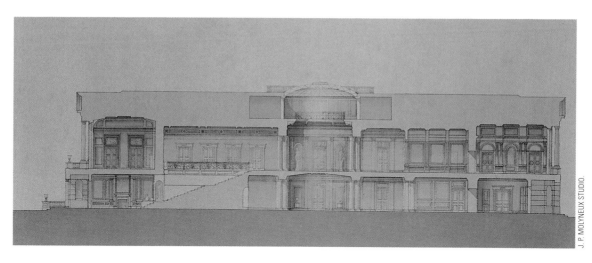

J. P. MOLYNEUX STUDIO

Cross section of my project in Canada shows the proportions of each of the rooms. The overall rhythm of the spaces and their relationship with each other are very important.

There is a wonderful sentence about Gabriel's work in the old *Encyclopedia Britannica*. It says that his architecture was esteemed for its elegance "in an age that regarded elegance as commonplace." That in itself is a very Gabriel-like encapsulation, because his work is very much like that: a little more elegant than everyone else's, with gestures that retain their impact today.

Gabriel was a master of open space. In what would turn out to be the monarchy's last flurry of urban planning, Louis XV launched an archi-tectural campaign that brought new squares to Rennes, Rouen, Reims, Bordeaux, and finally Paris. For Paris, where a piece of land had been picked out along the Seine, he held a competition. There were 28 entries, and none pleased the discerning king, so he turned to his trusted Gabriel and in 1753 told him to take what was best from all the designs and make one of his own. I like the idea of this kind of amalgamation; it too sums up Gabriel's strength, his openness, and his practicality.

The square, which was first known as the Place Louis XV, was originally conceived to display an equestrian statue of the king as a Roman emperor. In 1792 it was renamed the Place de la Révolution and had a busy guillotine—almost 3,000 people were executed there, including, in 1793, Louis XVI. Eventually the obelisk from

OPPOSITE: *The Molyneux residence. The enfilade of rooms shown is typical of Gabriel's layout. The neoclassical door casing opens onto a very strict barrel-vaulted gallery. The gallery ceiling is a modern interpretation of a battle scene by Le Brun.* PHOTO: BILLY CUNNINGHAM.

Rendering showing my version of Gabriel's library at Versailles. I have changed several of his ideas, yet kept respectful to the spirit of his room.

Luxor became its centerpiece, and it was given the name by which it is known today, the Place de la Concorde.

Rather than turning his back on the Seine, or trying to appropriate it in any kind of contrived way, Gabriel embraced its soft movement as one of his façades. He crossed the square with two axes. The one that ends in the Madeleine he flanked with a pair of buildings—today the Hôtel Crillon and the Admiralty—that I think of as the most striking entrance and exit to the city. They are like a pair of beautiful andirons to a fire: perfectly scaled, impeccably detailed, they support and frame the great urban dance. As for the other axis, it cuts through the Tuileries, ending in a palace, the Louvre, on one side and drawing the eye through a park, the Champs Elysées, on the other.

Why is this square such a success; why does it inspire so? It's the combination of disparities: the buildings and the open space, the stillness and the movement, the solid ground and the water. All of these Gabriel linked together without resorting to the tactics of a typical square. In a typical square, all is closed in. In this square, in every direction, even where there are buildings, there is openness, there are vistas, there is an expansive—I would say even ebullient—sense of personality and vitality and life.

Now here is the point where you expect me to relate Gabriel's work more specifically to my own. Ah, the literalness—and the hubris—of the endeavor! But it is built into this kind of reflection, isn't it, the idea that you might make even a small link . . . and so, very gently, I might mention a rather elaborate project, a neoclassical small palace or we could say manoir that I have been working on for the last two years in the Canadian wilderness. What might I have taken from Gabriel's Place Louis XV here? The idea, I would probably say, is that you must always embrace and understand your setting. In my case, the owner had already situated the structure on top of a hill and created a

parterre—itself, in this context, a square of sorts—with a bridge that leads to a lake and allées that lead to a chapel on one side and an obelisk on the other. Even in remote Canada you must guide and please the eye, respond to the landscape, attune your building to its place in the world. My reaction, when I first saw the project, was that it was really in the spirit of Gabriel, and I have found great satisfaction in being a vital part of it.

Now back to Gabriel. Let's look at one of his façades. At the Ministère de la Marine (the Admiralty), Gabriel gave great thought to the experience of the passersby. He believed, as I certainly do, that the elevation of a building tells a story, and if it is a good story it will tell us about the inside of the building. At the Admiralty Gabriel is a kind of raconteur. He is a reporter on the past, on all the beauty of ancient Greece and Rome, the shapes and images and ornaments he saw on his *voyage en Italie.* You see this in most every building he does—it is a very *dixhuitième* idea to tell a story in this way. This explains his use of pediments with narratives, his statues, his entablatures, all arrayed and detailed with such grace and elegance and gusto. One knows, in an instant, that this is a building of some purpose and significance and that it has a hierarchy of rooms, uses, even behaviors, within.

In Canada I am speaking some of this same language. It is, for me, the essential language of architecture and design—really of Western

A section of my Canadian project showing the rotunda-vestibule on the neoclassical building. The opening in the cupola is in trompe l'oeil.

Civilization. By knowing and absorbing the achievements of the past, you reach harmony, rhythm, and proportion, all of which are the central concerns for me in a building.

Let's end by looking at one of Gabriel's most accomplished interiors, his library for Louis XVI at Versailles. I think of this room as a master lesson. It is an interior that, for once, I can say directly inspired one of my own—the library for this manoir in Canada, which is of a similar concept, proportion, and purpose. Gabriel's library has height but no greed. Anyone other than this master would have gone all the way to the ceiling with books, for example; Gabriel instead makes a soffit, which humanizes the scale and allows him to apply moldings and carvings above. In my version, I reversed the soffit, extending it over the books rather than having it recede as Gabriel does; this allowed me to deal with a modern concern, lighting, which I was then able to wash over the books. Like Gabriel I've used gilded moldings and a parquet de Versailles floor, though I've rendered the room in mahogany.

But it's the Gabrielian *esprit* of this room that moves me so. In the vast palace of Versailles, he understood the need to change the rhythm, to seek out intimacy. And what better space than in a library? A library is personal, idiosyncratic, and human; it is of and about the man for whom the room was made. It is a space for retreat and reflection, for arranging private collections, for taking time to enter into just that conversation with the past that meant so much to the architect and designer in Jacques-Ange Gabriel and means so much to the architect and designer in me. It is a wonderful thing to be able to envision a great urban square, but in the scheme of human well-being an intimate, perfectly conceived, judiciously appointed library is as important, and hopefully, just as lasting.

Frank's interior of the Grand Salon dans l'hotel particulier du Vicomte Charles de Noailles as Frank had originally designed it in 1929.

Juan Montoya

~ *on* ~

JEAN-MICHEL FRANK

I have always been fascinated by materials, especially by the surface or skin of things. I like the play of one material next to another. In my work I frequently define one surface from another in a room by the contrast of material finish and texture: smooth is read against rough, shiny against matte, dark against light. I am also drawn to the shape of objects and their relationship to the spatial volume in which they exist.

In my youth, I had the great fortune to be invited by a friend to visit the eighteenth-century Beaux-Arts apartment building of the Vicomte de Noailles on the Place des Etats-Unis in Paris, the interior of which Jean-Michel Frank had designed in 1929–1930. This was my first exposure to the work of Frank. I was thunderstruck by the economy of the rooms—you could even say their emptiness—but also by their richness and sensuality achieved through the use of wonderful materials covering the walls and furniture. This was made even more apparent by experiencing the transition from leaving the eighteenth-century ornamentation of the building façade to entering these spare, clean rooms. Even though many decades had passed, Jean-Michel Frank's approach to the rooms was still so avant-garde, so completely unexpected, so exciting. I was intrigued by Frank's sense of space, by the number and proportion of the

Interior of the legendary Hotel Llao Llao (Bariloche Provincia de Rio Negro, Argentina) by architect Alejandro Bustillo and with furniture designed by J. M. Frank.

objects in that space, and by his use of extraordinary materials. The monochromatic living room was almost austere in its sparseness, yet extraordinarily rich with its high walls sheathed in vellum; monumental bronze doors with ivory details; oversized sofa and chairs in bleached leather; and tables and screens covered in shagreen, vellum, and lacquer. Here I felt relaxed and at the same time very creatively fulfilled. Even though I didn't fully realize it then, this experience was pivotal in its influence on my

own work. Although the vicomte and vicomtesse had long passed on, I was very grateful that their heirs at that point in time still maintained the apartment unchanged.

Jean-Michel Frank's life was rich as it was tragic. Two of his brothers were killed in World War I; his father committed suicide; and his mother died in an asylum four years later. Frank himself committed suicide in 1941 at only 46 years of age. After his mother's death Frank found himself with a sizable inheritance that enabled him to cruise the world for five years aboard luxury steamships.

Frank met one of his first mentors in 1927: Madame Eugenia Errzauriz, an elderly, intermittently rich Chilean who had come to Europe in the 1880s. Frank at the time was only 32 years old and fascinated, to say the least, by Errzauriz's unique and individual sense of style—mixing the best of the old with the best of the new. The search for furnishings for his own apartment led him to the decorator Adolphe Chanaux, with whom he opened a salon at 140 rue du Faubourg Saint-Honoré. Their salon was visited regularly by the painter Christian Bérard, the architect Emilio Terry, and the sculptor Alberto Giacometti and his brother Diego, the designer.

Frank admired the architecture of Robert Mallett-Stevens and subscribed to his dictum that "you can most luxuriously install a room by unfurnishing it rather than furnishing it." It was most likely through Mallett-Stevens that Frank met the Noailles, who had hired Mallett-Stevens to design their modernist concrete country home at Hyères. The Vicomte Charles de Noailles and his wife, Marie-Laure, were widely known as patrons of the avant-garde, and the word spread that Frank had designed one of the most important interiors ever.

In 1939, Frank, who was Jewish, got word that the War was approaching and left Europe. He lived and worked with Ignacio Pirovano in Buenos Aires, and together with the Argentine architect Bustillo they designed the now leg-

PHOTO: SONIA, 1936.

The main drawing room walls are in vellum. The low tables are in shagreen and bronze; the chairs in white leather; the mantle pieces in gypsum.

endary Hotel Llao Llao. The hotel's furnishings were reminiscent of Frank's previous work— blocky, rectangular club chairs and sofas that were simply designed and covered with extraordinary materials.

A few years ago, I was visiting Buenos Aires and went to see the Hotel Llao Llao. Although the hotel is still in operation, regrettably it has been remodeled. It was a very nostalgic visit. Very recently, I was fortunate enough to purchase two original sofas that had been designed by Frank for the Llao Llao. I placed these sofas, along with many other wonderful pieces from this period, in a living room that I designed for a townhouse in New York City.

PHOTO: KOLLAR.

Drawing room mantelpiece in white marble. The lamps and mirror are by Diego and Alberto Giacometti. The carpet is by Bérard.

When I first started my career many years ago, I was captivated by industrial materials and how they could be used in residential interiors. I used vinyl for wall coverings and furniture upholstery, automobile paints to cover a foyer wall or an architectural element in a room, stainless steel for furniture and millwork, rubber flooring in a kitchen or a child's room, and glass and metal as found originally in hospitals and factories for wall dividers between a master bedroom and a dressing room. As time has passed, I have become more and more intrigued by materials from nature and their application in design. At the same time, my interest in the body of work of Jean-Michel Frank has grown and deepened. I have frequently remembered my visit to the Noailles apartment in Paris. The rooms reflected the veneer of natural materials rather than applied color or pattern or ornamentation. Walls were no longer covered in moldings and cornices. Instead, they were clad entirely with vellum, wood, leather, or straw. Frank's furniture was reduced to the most basic and logical form while being enveloped in a variety of rich and

Montoya Residence, New York. *Leather tufted dressers and a suede tufted upholstered wall rethink tradition.*

exotic materials found in nature. These materials included mica, parchment, shagreen, straw, gypsum, and vellum. While the forms were seemingly simple, they were and are today a celebration of luxurious natural materials. Frank was also innovative in the treatment of natural materials; oak, for example, could be sandblasted, gouged, pickled, or tooled over by a chisel or adze.

Today, in my own New York City apartment, I clad my bedroom wall in 18-by-18-inch panels of leather. I designed certain furniture pieces with the same material and pattern but in a smaller proportion. I was struck again by Jean-Michel Frank's work in the year 2000, when I visited the Biennale Des Antiquaires in Paris. At the booth of Passebon, I viewed the installation of an original room entirely covered

PHOTO: BILLY CUNNINGHAM.

Erlich Residence, New York. *A demonstration of symmetry and geometry using walls of parchment.*

in square leather panels designed by Jean-Michel Frank in the 1920s for a house in Paris. The room also had a wonderful limestone fireplace conceived by both Frank and Giacometti. From the very beginning, when I first opened my design firm in New York in 1978, I conceived my practice as a couture house of interior design. I am not wedded to a particular style or period—my client and the space dictate what style I will be working in. As with Frank, my rooms are never full and there is always the careful placement of objects and furniture to enhance the qualities of the space and scale in the room.

I consider myself a tailor who finds the best materials to clothe an interior in the most appealing and comfortable manner, down to the last detail. This is another element that intrigues me about Jean-Michel Frank. His eye for every fine detail and the craftsmanship to achieve that detail is without a doubt the finest I have ever seen. The spare forms of his aesthetic leave no room for a sloppy cut or stitch or edge. No superfluous molding or applied decoration could be employed to hide the lack of skill of the craftsman. Frank worked very closely with his craftsmen to achieve the finest of detail; I continue to do the same today with the many wonderful artisans with whom I have the great fortune to do my work.

This fascination with nature that I share with Jean-Michel Frank has manifested itself in many different ways and has led me to use many materials that are found in my native Colombia. For instance, I have discovered many uses for tagua, a seed pod that grows on trees in my homeland and carves and veneers like ivory. The native Indians have used it for a variety of objects for centuries. Today in Colombia you can purchase many products carved from tagua—for example, necklaces and bracelets, as well as items for the home like drawer pulls and doorknobs. I also have sources in Colombia where I buy the raw natural material so that I can have local craftspeople carve things that I have designed. I

Private residence, Paris. *A restrained and subtly dramatic room using parchment walls, rich woods, and leather.*

have also created many furniture pieces covered in materials found in South America, including a variety of woods and leathers.

Today I continue to search for interesting materials throughout the world, and I experiment with their application to interior design. My design studio is a laboratory for experimentation with a variety of materials. As they were for Jean-Michel Frank, natural materials continue to be a great source of my inspiration.

Hall painted on slates, inspired by Monsú Desiderio's painting as designed by Renzo Mongiardino.

Roberto Peregalli

~ *on* ~

RENZO MONGIARDINO

It is difficult for me to speak about Renzo Mongiardino for two reasons. First of all, he was one of the most famous, and at the same time most secretive, masters of the last century (Mongiardino was born in Genoa in 1916 and died in Milan in 1998). Second, I knew him all his life and was also his pupil.

Mongiardino could be defined as a creator of rooms, of sites. In a contradictory century, in which the most daring examples of Art Nouveau were being replaced and supplanted by the masterpieces of conceptual abstractionism, he created an unassuming and difficult link with a more distant past, ranging from the remotest forms of classicism all the way down to the dazzling and nostalgic decadentism of the nineteenth century.

He worked with the assurance and coolness of an artisan, uninfluenced by the appeal of passing fashions or myths. In every site, his aim was to create a harmony of effects that would provide a familiar atmosphere—the proustian reminiscence of minor factors—like a ray of light reflected on a wall, the simple design of a bookcase, the breathtaking amazement before an unusual height, the texture of a fabric. He believed that in architecture everything was possible, provided that the approach chosen created the overall harmony that every site should have.

PHOTO: MASSIMO LISTRI.

Small breakfast room by Roberto Peregalli and partner Laura Sartori Rimini with vaulted ceiling, with a decoration giving the impression of a tent; Lombard table of the late eighteenth century; antique cotto tiles on the floor.

Renzo Mongiardino's dining room with eighteenth-century stucco panels, light blue and ivory, arranged in order to form the walls.

In any case, a natural inclination toward the past is inherent in the human mind. Rilke expresses this in a beautiful elegy, as well as Hölderlin, Nietzsche, and Heidegger. It is like a light, a flash of something that lies beyond our immediate perception. The impossibility of dis- regarding the past seems clearly part of human destiny. In a historicistic time such as ours, the past is imprisoned in a shrine, to be admired but not to be made use of. It is worshiped, it is pol- ished up (restoration work frequently represents a betrayal rather than an act of love for the original), but it can never be imitated. Mongiardino, on the contrary, believed that the past is all we have; it is the reminiscence of the world that forged us and that, as such, can be freely stolen from and drawn upon in an attempt, perhaps, to break new ground.

In 1978, when I asked him if studying philosophy, as I had planned to do, would have interfered with focusing on the work I was carrying out with him, he said no, it wouldn't, that I would probably be more disturbed by the principles of modern architecture that I would otherwise have studied. At first, I considered this merely a polemical remark, which was quite understandable in a person who for 40 years had been working counter to the general trend. I

Renzo Mongiardino's living room with a barrel-vaulted ceiling coming down to the floor, panels in trompe l'oeil of Russian inspiration.

Large living room/ballroom with a complex architectural decoration, with columns and trompe l'oeil of perspectives and greenery; large skylight in the middle as designed by Renzo Mongiardino.

reconsidered the question at length subsequently, during my work with him, and then even later, when I was engaged in creating the small spaces or sites which rooms represent.

The first point to be considered involves the concept of freedom. In Mongiardino's way of thinking, there are no preconceived ideas. There is merely a site to be created, what it means to us as human beings, and what our ancestors can teach us. There is no scale of importance between different rooms: they are all equally important. A dining room, a hall, a staircase, a bathroom are reflections of something deeply rooted in the personality of the occupant.

The second point involves the concept of rigor. In art there are no formal constrictions, provided it complies with clearly defined rules. The fundamentals of architecture, from its earliest days in ancient Egypt and ancient Greece, are based on modules, susceptible to unlimited variations, as long as their essence is not changed. For instance, a column and its trabeat- ion may have different styles or dimensions, but they cannot be replaced or their roles inverted. The appeal of what is considered ugly, codified by Hegel in the nineteenth century and carried to the extreme in the last century, is fading. Dissimilarity and discordance cannot become the rule. Choosing to skip this period, as far as its most conspicuous aspects are concerned, does

Roberto Peregalli and partner Laura Sartori Rimini's large room with bed; stucco and walls frescoed to represent Pompeian ruins; fake mosaic painted on wooden floor; nineteenth-century iron camp bed.

not imply on Mongiardino's part a nostalgic revival of the past, but a need for rigor.

The third point, trickier and more subtle, regards the concept of style. Mongiardino's projects, and his sketches or models (often "no bigger than a cigarette case," as he used to say, and yet not lacking in completeness), which he conceived and pondered at length, when carefully examined reveal an overall and coherent view, subsequently segmented in a close and intricate network, deeply rooted in the present, in an attempt to find the meaning of each constituent part and give a name to the sometimes frayed design of contemporary architecture.

In addition, as certain musicians choose to devote years to developing variations on similar themes based on just one instrument, likewise, in pursuing this concept of modern architecture, Mongiardino focused on rooms. His work gives us a bewildering feeling of dizziness before the infinite possibility of signs in a tiny universe, which Pascal perceived as the sign of the infinite universe. It is not a question of size, but of depth. To give an example, an immensely tall curtain falling in a double fold over the sides of a cube reveals the vertiginous potential of a body, expressed in its deepest essence.

A broken-down, crumbling piece of architecture, painted on a wall, reminiscent of Clérisseau and Piranesi, as well as of rediscovered ancient Roman ruins, outlines the dimension of a small room in an inaccessible tower. A gigantic fireplace, similar to an impudent sea god or a

View of the living room from the dining room; dining room in red lacquer–painted stucco with Indian patterns; the walls of the living room are in golden wood, painted with Oriental patterns reminiscent of ancient Japanese screens as designed by Roberto Peregalli and partner Laura Sartori Rimini.

fearful Gorgon, endows it with mythical purport: a superhuman cameo that conceals the intimate significance of the project. The apparent discordance between the gigantic and the tiny elements is played down in the harmonious synthesis of an imaginary landscape.

PHOTO: MASSIMO LISTRI

A large living room by Roberto Peregalli and partner Laura Sartori Rimini with Renaissance patterns on frescoed faded walls; stucco paneled ceiling and nineteenth-century Ushak carpets.

And then, as in a dream, this is followed by a brick grotto, the perspective holes of which reveal open spaces and shapes, walls overrun with creepers in an oppressive, protoromantic revenge of nature, a painted balcony looking out on an imaginary city—apparently a chaos of different styles but in fact a harmonious superimposing of Renaissance and Neorenaissance, with a scrupulous outline of skyscrapers.

In the plain decoration of this room, Mongiardino conceived, as Boullée and Ledoux had done in the past, ideal cities—imaginary shapes in which past, present, and future are knit together in a unitarian view ranging from the austere, jutting profiles of San Gimignano to the futuristic outlines of a phantasmagoric New York. His rooms reverberate one after the other like visionary images. They represent the story of a dream of architecture. The clearness of this dream and its naturalness are intimately connected.

Following the example of classic masters, in particular Leonbattista Alberti and Donato Bramante, he believed that the importance of a project was not its dimension, but its infinite complexity, regardless of whether it involved a box, a staircase, a room, a building, or a city. And he threw himself into the enterprise, analyzing all its possibilities. Unlike the principles inherent in modern architectural design, no consideration was ever given to the industrial serializing of his projects. Each item or site had a life of its own, dependent on the situation, the light, and the climate. The quality of his work was set in this theoretical framework. In his view, a frame, a coating, the fringe for a sofa, the size of a window represented equivalent problems, each to be dealt with and to be solved.

Architecture, theatre, cinema, the design of a piece of furniture were part of his creative universe. They constituted the link between reality and creative fantasy. For Mongiardino, conceiving scenery or real sites was part of the same ideal of the imaginative planning skill that enabled both to draw from the same fount.

PHOTO: MASSIMO LISTRI.

Important dining room by Roberto Peregalli and partner Laura Sartori Rimini painted in fake malachite with ivory and ochre edgings; a collection of eighteenth-century dishes; a nineteenth-century chandelier.

Every time I look at Mongiardino's projects, I feel that this "obstetrician" of architectural art, as Socrates calls the human mind, gave birth through his work to the minute texture of a plot in which abstract ideas develop into actual potentialities, like the forge of a magician who reveals the secrets of his work in the act of creating.

PHOTO: DERRY MOORE.

Elsie de Wolfe's drawing room at her Villa Trianon in Versailles attests to her passion for mirrors. The banquette is lined with blue pillows embroidered with her favorite sayings, including "There are no pockets in a shroud."

Suzanne Rheinstein

~ on ~

ELSIE DE WOLFE

The Villa Trianon captured me completely the moment I saw photographs of it. Full of light and beautiful objects and furniture, it was Elsie de Wolfe's version of eighteenth-century French perfection. For her, it was in the tradition of those rarified retreats built for themselves by women who adored furniture and houses, such as Isabella d'Este and the Marquise de Rambouillet.

The villa was acquired in the early 1900s and renovated with Elsie's friends Elisabeth Marbury and Anne Morgan. Though in the Park of Versailles, it was very different from the chateau, which Elsie considered ugly and vulgar. *Their* villa was going to embody what Elsie

called "the three genies of the fairy whose name is Good Taste—Simplicity, Suitability and Proportion." Although it meant furnishing the place slowly, they determined that they would buy only wonderful things—and what wonderful things they bought! Elsie writes in *After All* (Harper, 1935), her autobiography, about buying the ancient boiseries for the salons from her American mentor, Minna, Lady Anglesly. After the whitewash was scraped off, she was left with beautiful blue-and-white paneling, which became the inspiration for the color scheme in the salons. She also bought old hand-woven silk curtains in blue and white for the windows—and when, many years later, they disintegrated,

PHOTO: DERRY MOORE.

Elsie de Wolfe's famous bathroom as a sitting room at the Villa Trianon.

she commissioned someone who spent a year and a half patiently recreating them.

When she had perfected the architecture and backgrounds, I loved the way Elsie filled the salon with chic low banquettes, perfect for perching at her many parties. I have always loved Directoire and Louis XVI chairs as graphic objects of beauty, as places to sit, and as party props to easily move from one conversation to the next. The fauteuils in Elsie's salon, as you might imagine, were the best.

She had a sense of playfulness, too. Embroidered in small letters on plain silk satin pillows

were her aphorisms. Her most famous was, "Never explain. Never complain." My favorite is, "There are no pockets in a shroud." These pillows were neatly lined up against the banquettes at the villa and in all her houses. During the years of World War II, at her house in Beverly Hills, also called "After All," the pillows would be dark green silk satin.

At the Villa Trianon, the paintings and drawings, all of different sizes, were hung vertically on the boiserie panels and organized by charming trompe l'oeil cords and tassels from which they seemed to hang. Elsie de Wolfe had very particular ideas on hanging art. "One cannot be too careful about pictures," she wrote, warning against the "unrest" caused by "amateur oil paintings" defacing a surface or small pictures dotted around a bedroom. "Unrest," she noted, could also be stirred up by "gewgaws all over the place . . ." or ". . . a regiment of inconsequentials . . . that peck at the nerves." How true! In the villa there were rare and beautiful objects: a coral pagoda, a Fabergé clock, a tiny sixteenth-century unicorn that was her talisman—displayed with restraint. Elsie believed that the cardinal virtue of all beauty is restraint.

Light mattered to her enormously. The villa was airy and welcomed sunshine in the daytime. At night, here and at all her houses, girandoles and candlesticks were everywhere. Don't we all agree that lighted candles—and lots of them— are essential for making a house magical at night? Elsie used only antique lighting fixtures

COURTESY OF CHARLOTTE MOSS.

A watercolor painting of the eighteenth-century-style music pavilion at the Villa Trianon. Painted for Elsie's personal collection by William Rankin.

at the villa, and had them electrified in such a way that even they seemed like candlelight.

She loved to light the garden, too, and experimented with soft lighting that seemed like moonlight. The garden was all green architecture; my very favorite kind of garden. After she planted the box mazes, there were no flowers to be seen from the terrace. Low box borders, clipped yews, Tuscan pines, and old and weath-ered statuary created a vista whichever way one might look. A potager, cutting beds, and greenhouses were hidden in garden "rooms."

In the back of our city house in Los Angeles, my husband and I have a small, crisp, clipped green garden, which never fails to delight us. In contrast, and hidden away, are a small lush cutting garden and a pool garden of tropical plants and citrus in tubs. We do put out

Entrance hall, Hobe Sound, Florida by Suzanne Rheinstein. Fancifully hand-painted sun on painted wooden floor, eighteenth century. French furniture and white flowers show Elsie's influence.

large pots of yellow clivia in winter and ones of hydrangeas in the summer, as we are less disciplined than Elsie and can't resist.

In the back of the green garden at the Villa Trianon, Elsie built a music pavilion. It was of treillage in eighteenth-century style, octagonal, with high ceilings and an old floor, of the sort that once stood in the Park of Versailles. When it was filled with beautiful people sitting on the eighteenth-century chairs and musicians playing eighteenth-century music, and there were swans gliding upon the pool, at least one guest described it as a fairyland.

In the early years of the twentieth century, Elsie created her famous Trellis Room at the Colony Club, the first in this country. Airy and elegant, fresh in winter and cool in summer, it inspired a vogue in America for lovely trellised sunrooms and loggias. Soon after, she designed a chic trellised winter garden for Mrs. Ogden Armour in Lake Forest, near Chicago. She used her favorite color scheme of green and white with black-and-white marble floors. At one point, trellis rooms were everywhere, but I hope now that enough time has passed so that they have gone from cliché to classic. I love them done with painted trompe l'oeil, perhaps in a sunroom. I still love the Mauny papier paint of treillage. I, like Elsie, think it is attractive to use real trellis in a garden, but only if the building, fence, or screen is carefully constructed. The slapdash thin trellis panels available at garden centers are better left there!

PHOTO: TIM STREET-PORTER.

A corner of a living room by Suzanne Rheinstein, Los Angeles, with the crystal, slipcovers, and fauteuils Elsie advocated.

Elsie introduced other notions at the Colony Club, which seemed startling. The idea of using chintz in public rooms, rather than more elaborate silks and brocades, was one. I liked the way she upholstered French fauteuils with chintz, with the chair acting as a painted frame. I have always been mad about old painted furniture. Chintzes that are hand blocked, or hand screened, are beautiful. So nat-

PHOTO: TIM STREET-PORTER.

Suzanne Rheinstein's powder room, Los Angeles. With the rock crystal sconces, old mirror, and eighteenth-century French pictures that Elsie loved.

urally, I would like the two of them together, trying to remember Elsie's admonition of restraint.

Slipcovers are favorites of mine. They allow you to have two different looks in one room, or to make furniture a little more relaxed (not sloppy!) than close upholstery. I assumed that they had been around forever, and they may have been, but Elsie said she popularized them in this country. There were part of her fresh look and her attempts to do away with the fusty American interior.

I love the high glamour look of Elsie, too, the one that permeated her fabulous Paris apartment on the rue d'Iena. This look is exemplified by satin quilted in intricate designs for headboards and bedspreads, throws of chinchilla, more beautiful objects—old birds on hunks of rock crystal—more candlelight, and white orchids rather than the bowls of flowers in the country.

The famous, favorite room on the rue d'Iena was the bathroom. It was like a grand salon. "All moonshine and glamour," said Elsie. The curtains were thin silver lamé. Around the room was a frieze of mirrors painted with Venus and Neptune, waves, and other symbols associated with the sea. A mirrored mantelpiece, glowing with firelight, was adorned with paintings of shells; even the light sconces were made of oyster shells. A long low banquette was covered in zebra skin and the rug was white velvet. White flowers only—roses, lilies, and tuberoses—filled the room. Elsie said she marked the seasons by the flowers in this room. After a while, Miss West, Elsie's loyal secretary, and Miss West's desk moved in. Elsie reigned from there.

For me, Elsie's bathroom at the Villa Trianon would be the spot. Collections of quirky reverse glass paintings were hung over the flower-patterned walls. In one corner there is a beautiful marble fireplace, and in another an antique encoignure fitted with taps and a basin. There are delicious old chairs in which to sit, and a red chinoiserie screen to hide behind.

In his memoir of Elsie, *To the One I Love Best*, Ludwig Bemelmans writes about staying at After All, and of his difficulty in figuring out that the bathroom was indeed the bathroom! Completely cosseting, the room had a desk for working, a daybed for napping, and a curtain that drew back to reveal a tub with pillows, bath rack, and lots of magazines to read while soaking. Always, the unmentionable, unspeakable porcelain monstrosity was hidden.

In California, Elsie's own bathroom walls were sheathed in panes of shadowed mirrors. Again, there was a long low banquette in darkest green and white, the colors of the house. There were white goatskin rugs on the floor, silver frames, an ormolu clock, and long stemmed lilies. Here, Bemelmans conjures up an 80-year-plus Elsie, in a pale turban with a vicuna and satin blanket.

After All hadn't the architectural bones of her other houses, so she transformed it with bold gestures and a color scheme of black, white, and dark green. There were green striped canvas curtains at the entrance, a wide striped tented ceiling in the dining room, and abundant use of her famous fern print, which is still popular and fresh.

In this house were some of the spectacular things that Elsie commissioned from the now famous Tony Duquette: twisting consoles, feather frames, elegant dressed figures, and an inspired "mueble" as she called the fabulously decorated secretary that was returned to Duquette's Dawnridge house in Beverly Hills after Elsie's death.

I think it must have been at Tony's house that I first experienced the glamour and exoticism of rock crystal and coral constructions and pagodas made of anything, although, in contrast to Elsie's famous restraint, Tony liked to say, "More is more."

Although she was frail and old, Elsie left Beverly Hills after World War II and returned to her beloved house in France to begin anew. She wanted to make it come alive, bringing to it all she knew from instinct and worldly travels about the way to live. She never gave up.

Betty Sherrill

~ *on* ~

ELEANOR BROWN

Eleanor McMillen Brown was my employer for 30 years, and my mentor. She was renowned for her taste, yes. But she also believed in a disciplined approach to design—specifically, in the harmony of line, color, proportion, and feeling. She had vision, and she had integrity. In that she created a firm of decorators, she set standards for decoration in America as a profession.

I first met Mrs. Brown in the fall of 1949 at the Parsons School of Design in New York City. I was a beginning student, and she was speaking to our class in a soft, rather timid voice—a bit hard to hear. Mrs. Brown was at least a generation older than I was. As I remember, she was wearing a dark suit with white piping, and had on white gloves, as she always did.

Mrs. Brown was describing to the class how she had closed up two huge windows of a living room that overlooked Central Park West. I was a bit taken aback to think of anyone doing something like that, but as I listened, I began to realize that Mrs. Brown was brilliant, and that I intended to work for her at McMillen as soon as possible.

Mrs. Brown would not hire me when I first asked for a job. One of the standards she had set at McMillen was that each of her employees had to have finished a course of professional training, preferably at Parsons. Finally, however, I wore her down. This was partly because I was determined to work for her, partly because certain McMillen clients had spoken to her on my behalf, and partly because of luck. At the moment I was (again) asking her for a job, Mrs. Brown happened to have been giving an exhibition for Art Deco designers from France (I remember one of them was Poillerat), and she needed someone who would be willing to stand in the doorway of the McMillen townhouse and hand out the exhibition pamphlets. My career at McMillen, and my relation with Mrs. Brown, was definitely a validation of the truth of the old adage, "Just get your foot in door"—in this case, literally.

Mrs. Brown started in the business of design for somewhat the same reason I did. We were both living in New York—not our native city—and looking for something to do. Although I was not divorced, as Mrs. Brown was, I was homesick for New Orleans, and I cried every day. I had always been interested in decorating—first my

PREVIOUS SPREAD: *Living room from Colonel H.H. Rogers's "Port of Missing Men," Southampton, New York. McMillen's interior decoration reflects the owner, a sportsman and a collector of model ships and marine paintings. A rack of guns lines one wall, leather fire buckets align the fire mantel, and a miniature replica of the* Juno, *an eighteenth-century ship originally owned by Admiral Jackson of the British Navy, is suspended from the ceiling. Timber beams and rough plaster walls are softened by hooked rugs and henna/red linen sofas, creating a room that is both interesting and inviting.*

room, and then our house. My mother finally let me pick out my own bed and put up wallpaper borders in the attic. When my family had to live for a year in the Roosevelt Hotel across from Canal Street, I used to wander around in the French quarter every afternoon by myself, looking into antique shops. (I think that's how I learned to spot reproduction French furniture from a long way away—from looking at it in windows.) I particularly loved porcelain, especially Dresden, although I loved it more then than I do now.

Therefore, when I found myself lonely again, this time in New York, the idea of decorating presented itself as a solution, and I began taking courses at Parsons and calling myself "Elizabeth Sherrill, Interiors"—because I thought Elizabeth, which was not my name, sounded more serious than Betty, the name I was christened with.

As to Mrs. Brown's beginnings in design, I have always understood that she became interested merely because a friend of hers who was taking courses at Parsons called the New York School of Fine and Applied Arts and suggested that Mrs. Brown come along. I do not believe that Mrs. Brown had ever considered a career in design before that point, but it was a sign of her innate talent that her possibilities were immediately recognized by Frank Alvah Parsons, the head of the New York School of Fine and Applied Arts, and by William Odom, the director of the Paris branch of the school. In fact, Mrs. Brown, then still Eleanor McMillen, had been such a favorite of Mr. Parsons and Mr.

A paneled bedroom with original American furniture and decoration in Colonel H.H. Rogers's "Port of Missing Men" Southampton, New York. A canopy bed with a tasseled net tester, an old appliqué quilt, and blue-and-red patterned hooked rugs grace this room. Architecture by John Russell Pope; interior design by McMillen.

Odom that for years her name was held up to students as an example of the school's success. This happened to such an extent that it became a joke among the students. "What will you do when you graduate?" they would ask one another. And each would answer, "Why, I shall work for Eleanor McMillen!"

Mrs. Brown's father, who had founded the Magic Chef Stove Co., established her in New York after her divorce and sent her money with which to attend design school. When she decided to go into business, at the suggestion of William Odom and with his encouragement (basically, as his partner—she sold French furniture for him in New York), her father bought her two townhouses—one to live in and one for her office—and insisted that before beginning her profession, she attend business classes.

Unlike Mrs. Brown's situation, there were no men in my life, particularly in my family, who

ELIZABETH HOOPES/COURTESY OF MCMILLEN, INC.

Watercolor of living room of Eleanor McMillen Brown and Archibald Brown, Southampton, NY. Originally a theater with a stage, it was transformed into a splendid living/dining room. A Raoul Dufy tapestry, a bold patterned rug, and a sofa filled the huge dramatic space (40-feet square), with Italian and French chairs arranged for intimate conversations.

thought it was proper for me to have a job—especially not my father, though he himself had taught me much about design and about the beauty of objects, as he was a trained architect. It was actually my mother-in-law who sent me money for

courses at Parsons, and it was Mrs. Brown's example that suggested to me the possibility of being a professional—a "serious" professional.

I never heard Mrs. Brown laugh too loudly, and I never heard her cry. She was totally differ-

Betty Sherrill's living room, Hobe Sound, Florida. The cool but comfortable living room has a tile floor throughout. A zebra rug adds zip—as do colorful pillows and throws and of course flowers—to the neutral upholstery grouped around a view of the water.

ent from my mother, who loved long-stemmed American Beauty roses (Mrs. Brown's favorite flower was the anemone) and tried to run away from the family plantation when she was 16, galloping on a horse toward Houston.

Mrs. Brown wrote to me once when I was ill that I was the daughter she never had, and I keep that letter in a little drawer by my bed. I learned a lot from my mother, but I also learned from Mrs. Brown—her discipline, her restraint,

and her balance, whether in her decisions or in her sense of design. As a person and as a designer, she seems to me to have been totally infused with the spirit of the neoclassical, which was her favorite period as well.

Mrs. Brown was a total professional. I think this differentiated her from the other women of her generation in design. When she decided to open her business, she set up her company with a business office and a separate department for

COURTESY OF MCMILLEN, INC.

Betty Sherrill's living room, New York. Yellow, "the color of sunlight," with intimate seating groups. The decor has hardly changed throughout the years.

architectural drafting. This made McMillen the first full-service, structured design firm, which it still is today.

Mrs. Brown was intensely loyal to her employees—whether they were administrators or the designers she had been in school with at Parsons—and she recognized from the begin-

ning that she needed to surround herself with the most talented designers she could find. Grace Fakes, a classmate of Mrs. Brown's in the Paris Atelier of Parsons in the Place des Vosges, worked in the design department at McMillen for more than 40 years, as did Marion Morgan, another classmate from Parsons; and Ethel Smith, a Parsons graduate of 10 or so years later, worked at McMillen from 1929 until she retired in 1999. All three women, like Mrs. Brown, were trained in the same disciplined way. Theirs was not a practical course that involved learning the difference between a silk and a satin. It was based on the history of art and architecture, and the days in the Paris Atelier and in trips around Europe were spent measuring the cornices and the moldings of the hotels of the ancien regime, chateaux, and Italian estates.

During the Depression Mrs. Brown made a commitment not to lay off any of her employees, and I have always been moved by her sacrifice in making sure that that did not happen. When we have been in difficult times today in our country, I have tried to keep Mrs. Brown's example in my mind. The length of time for which employees have worked at McMillen was unique in design firms, and I think it still is. The three principles of our firm today—Luis Rey, Mary Louise Guertler, and Katherine McCallum—have been at McMillen for 30, 40, and 20 years, respectively (and myself, 50 years). Although Mrs. Brown insisted that McMillen came first, the members of her firm always had their own

Betty Sherrill's wood paneled library, Dean Johnson residence, New York. Colorful chintz fabric brightens up the warm paneled library. The result is a delightful harmony between the feminine elements and the classical, more masculine elements of this room.

clients, and, as her firm evolved, Mrs. Brown treated them as independent designers, not as her assistants.

In many ways, Mrs. Brown was not a social person, but she entertained beautifully. She preferred small dinners of 8 to 10 guests, whom one always felt were chosen very carefully. I have

been accused of having one or two of what people might call "town sweeps," but such an event was never something Mrs. Brown would have considered.

Sometimes Mrs. Brown had flowers on the table, sometimes just a beautiful crystal bowl filled with lemons, the color of Mrs. Brown's

~ 147

Betty Sherrill's spiral stair, Dean Johnson residence, New York. A classic elegance is achieved as the beautiful iron railing accented by the black baseboard gracefully rises from the black and white marble floor. Together with the softer elements of this space—the Gracie Chinese wallpaper, the cream carpet, the draped table, the painted French chair upholstered in green— the stair appears both airy and solid.

PHOTO: PETER VITALE.

dining room during all the years she lived in New York. Mrs. Brown always said that yellow is a good color for rooms in the city, because it is the color of the sun and brings in so much light and warmth, which might otherwise be lacking. My own living room in New York is yellow, as is my living room in Southampton.

Mrs. Brown's house in Southampton had been a theatre before Mrs. Brown and her second husband, the architect Archibald Brown, renovated it. In theory, it represented a difficult design problem. It had to be appropriated for social use without its contents seeming too small in relation to the room's scale (the main room is 40 feet square; its ceiling is 20 feet). To solve the problem, Mrs. Brown hung a large silk Raoul Dufy, "Le Cirque," and used a boldly patterned rug and a spirited pattern on the sofa. But she also used refined eighteenth-century open armchairs and created intimate seating groups. I loved being in that room with her, chatting after a Sunday lunch, and when I was in the room I always admired her ability to understand scale and proportion. Perhaps as a result of my exposure to Mrs. Brown, the layout of a room is the first thing I consider, before color or even the feeling of a room.

Mrs. Brown had a perfect sense of scale and proportion. This must have been what brought her to the notice of Frank Alvah Parsons and William Odom and caused them to promote her. It was certainly what was emphasized in the Parsons curriculum at that time.

Mrs. Brown liked to use colors that were clear and strong—unsaturated. She used color with restraint, but very deliberately. Stylistically, she preferred the straight lines of the Louis XVI period and of early neoclassical Italian furniture. In her dining room in New York she created plaster niches that she filled with Greco-Roman statues, and in her living room she installed pilasters. Mrs. Brown believed that if the architecture of a room was designed correctly from the start, the decoration of the room would follow and would never have to be rethought.

But Mrs. Brown could work easily with any period, and mixing furniture from the different periods was always her strength. She always said that there was nothing more trite than recreating a period room. Of course, others of her generation, like Elsie de Wolfe or Rose Cumming, decorated eclectically. They did it with a lot of flair. But Mrs. Brown's eclecticism was very intellectual. What was important to her was the relation between object, size, form, texture, color, and meaning—regardless of what period an object was from. She used chintz rather sparingly. Her work was more severe than that of most of her contemporaries.

From my first introduction to Mrs. Brown as she spoke at Parsons, I knew that she was brilliant. I knew I could never compete with that, and so I never tried. Maybe someone might say my rooms are less formal and more comfortable than Mrs. Brown's—though of course they are of a different time and age.

In a letter written to me, Mitchell Owens of the *The New York Times* says, "Eleanor McMillen Brown gave us standards. She taught America that elegance can exist without pretension, that lightness doesn't mean frivolity; that the success of a room depends as much upon its arrangement as on the splendor of its contents."

As I look back over my own career, I see all the ways in which Mrs. Brown and I are similar, and the ways we are different. I was influenced by Mrs. Brown's professional standards. I was influenced by her belief that a decor should last. I was influenced by her boldness in mixing objects and backgrounds from different periods. I was influenced by her sense of restraint, of always knowing just how much was right. Certainly, in personal ways and in professional ways, Eleanor McMillen Brown was right for me.

Betty Sherrill's master bedroom, Farb residence, Houston, Texas. Pink chintz covers the canopy bed, and several upholstered chairs and along with creamy carpets create a restful bedroom.

PHOTO: FELICIANO. COURTESY OF *HOUSE & GARDEN*.

Marjorie Shushan

~ on ~

KALEF ALATON

One of my first impressions of Kalef Alaton was his expressive hands. Long, thin, and elegant, they had a definite resemblance to the long hands in an El Greco painting. These hands explained, pointed, and rearranged an object or a room. It was sheer theater to watch those hands in motion, mesmerizing to all.

Kalef was born in Istanbul in 1940, and as a young teenager he was sent to be schooled in Paris and to live alone without family in a Parisian hotel. He once told me how he would often replace classroom studies with visits to museums, art galleries, historic houses, and even antique shops. Some days he would wander the Paris Marchéoupuce. I can almost see him walking the flea market and spotting a treasure in the most unlikely pile of junk. When this happened, I'm sure his smile, which I later became familiar with, was that of a child.

Through self-schooling and formal art school training he managed to transform his life. Leaving Europe in 1968, he settled in Los Angeles and with his classical education and the ease of California living he became recognized in the design world for a contemporary blend with a European style. What better place to combine his sense of opulence than the fantasy and landscape of Hollywood? Known for his Twenties Mediterranean style, he approached his projects as if he were the new curator appointed to revitalizing a musty museum. He used the finest of fabrics, clean backgrounds to exhibit treasures, modern upholstery, and antiques to make a room sing. Kalef Alaton loathed imitation, small objects, and cutting corners.

I was always amazed at how he could translate a design image: a touch of California glamour into a London Belgravian townhouse; the wondrous glow of a gold-leaf ceiling in a drawing room or a brilliant hunting pink upholstery for a Montecito weekend retreat with dark oak furniture and rough white plaster walls. The man from Istanbul could make the English feel at home in California.

I saw Kalef's work several times in *Architectural Digest* and, because I admired it so much, I recommended him to a close friend for his home in Aspen. I had no idea how this recommendation would change my life and impel me back into the design world, which I had so decidedly left when I moved from New Orleans to Aspen to change my lifestyle. My first introduction to Kalef was in 1978 when he visited my friend's project in Aspen. We became fast friends because we admired each other's work. After spending much time with him when he visited the project in Aspen, seeing the resulting enormous success of my friend's home, and having him constantly tell me, "You should definitely be back in the design world," Kalef's enormous confidence in me gave me the confidence to work with him as an associate during the remainder of his life.

Looking back through Kalef's published works one realizes how relevant he is to any designer today looking for inspiration. Good design is not opulence in and of itself. It really takes balance, stylishness, and a certain wit to achieve opulent design. Kalef's projects were always an emotional experience. His approach was to fall in love with the project and to stay in love long after the project was finished.

Kalef was bored with sameness. He wanted to create surprise, whether through juxtaposition of objects, blending of style, or simply the detailing of the laying of tile in an intriguing pattern. Upon reviewing some of his work, I came away once again with the feeling of an overall peaceful coexistence of diverse items from diverse places and periods of time. No single object grabbed center stage; rather, a bold blend created a harmonious whole.

He loved to share all his discoveries, and with his vast knowledge he was always eager to do so. His was not just a design career but also a career of life. He was always asking, "What's new?" in the many languages he spoke.

PREVIOUS SPREAD: *Kalef Alaton's entry, Los Angeles. Kalef loved the bare and uncluttered look. Here in his residence, he mixes classic furnishings with contemporary architecture. The floors are terra cotta tiles with a white concrete grid. The walls are white stucco. Again, we find an uncluttered look with elegance, which is what Kalef was all about.*

Private residence master bedroom, Dallas, Texas. This bedroom decorated by Kalef Alaton characterizes his scale and organized thoughts. Its monochromatic tones and unusual detail extend to furniture that includes an Indo-Portuguese mother-of-pearl cabinet, a Louis XVI–style game table, Italian gilt chairs, and even a Victorian rope stool.

His concept of formulating an interior was very much like the method of a superbly dressed lady: the perfect tailored suit or simple dress accessorized knowingly with the correct shoes and jewelry, all of the finest craftsmanship. His rooms reflected this approach. Scale was everything: handsomely proportioned upholstery accented with the treasures of the past or modern furniture of merit. Kalef Alaton enjoyed the game of decorating and invited his clients to participate. His clients became part of his life and were transformed by his irresistible view of the modern world. He always knew when it was time to encourage his clients to stop buying. He

Kalef Alaton's master bath, Los Angeles. Kalef's personal bathroom includes a sitting area. It is opulent and grand because of the fireplace and size, but still very elegant. There is a carved nineteenth-century marble mirror over the fireplace; a Russian armchair; and his collection of bronzes, ivories, and Roman glass bottles. Again one sees his mix of modern and classic elements.

wanted each project to have the balance that it needed with *appropriate* luxurious things, not just *more* luxurious things. His ultimate objective was to create glamorous environments, but ones that were ultimately to be lived in, not merely exercises in glitz.

Kalef's mind was like a sponge. He end-lessly read through design magazines, design and architectural books, and anything related to the world of design. When he needed a visual reference for a project, whether to convince a client or complete a presentation, he could go to the book or magazine he needed without hesitation. Needless to say, he had an

Private residence living room, Dallas, Texas. This room is another example of Kalef's organized simplicity with elegance that gave this Dallas residence a feeling of spaciousness. The calligraphic screens that flank the fireplace are the focal point of this room. Their size along with the bold black makes an important statement.

155

Marjorie Shushan's master bedroom, New York City. Marjorie Shushan always strives to achieve luxury and comfort in bedrooms. In her personal bedroom, she uses a canopy bed, good lighting, fine linens, and a cashmere throw at the foot of the bed. Marjorie feels all bedrooms should be tranquil.

PHOTO: SCOTT FRANCIS.

Private residence family room, Long Island, New York. This family room with its high ceiling and almost square dimensions allowed Shushan to use large-scale furniture. Antique wood was used to make the ceiling beams. A nineteenth-century Tuscan cabinet, a large black mirror that reflects the exterior, and the pine-paneled walls achieve a traditional atmosphere for a comfortable and relaxed retreat.

enormous library of design books, both in his office and his home.

Like his library, observations of the unique were carefully stored in his memory: a Flemish interior painting showing an oriental rug as a table covering with massive amounts of leather-bound books placed on top and a pewter plate laden with fruit, recreating a still life Vermeer would have envied—this idea was used in a California country house library.

Being a true romantic with a love of mystery, he would take great delight in surprising me with the unexpected: a magnificent candlelit dinner at the home of the Rothschilds—it was Paris at its peak; the following day, a flea market bistro with a newly discovered furniture

PHOTO: SCOTT FRANCIS.

Private residence entry, Long Island, New York. Shushan achieved an impressive but cozy feeling in this entry of a Hamptons house with 24-foot ceilings. The portieres on either side of the front door and at the French doors help to contain the room.

designer. For his clients his surprise might be silk hangings with Madagascar wall covering, Chinese lacquer with Venetian glass and sisal rugs, or bronzes on black granite tables.

His use of color was subtle. For example, the terra cotta of the tile floor would be echoed in a velvet pillow skipped over to a costume in an eighteenth-century portrait traveling to a dish of Turkish apricots; the color sienna never

looked so delicious. Kalef Alaton brought life to empty spaces, and everyone wanted to be a part of this romantic vision.

To this day, the spirit of Kalef whispers to me, "Marjorie, give them more beauty and a style of living that they did not dream possible. I promise they will recognize it." Sometimes when I return to a former project and discover how little the client has changed the interiors, I smile

PHOTO: SCOTT FRANCIS

Private residence dining room, Long Island, New York. In this Hamptons dining room Shushan uses a 10-foot walnut table from Rose Tarlow, chairs skirted to the wood floor, and a pair of antique bamboo demilune tables on either side of the fireplace. Pewter and iron are mixed with the contemporary service plates. Together these elements make this eclectic room warm and inviting.

and know, like Kalef, that I got it right the first time.

Kalef Alaton's presence is forever with me. I had complete faith in his enormous knowledge of the arts, and, given a problem of choice, still ask, "What would Kalef do?" The answer is always there: "Chose the best with discretion!"

My dear friend and mentor, Kalef Alaton, in his all-too-brief moments on this earth, managed to transform people and the places they inhabited. Nothing was ever ordinary for Kalef. He was always striving to do something different, something challenging, something that separated him from others. Kalef was unique and truly magical.

William Sofield

～ *on* ～

DONALD DESKEY

Throughout my academic training and continuing through the many evolutions of my career, I have always been most captivated and inspired by those heroic figures who occupy and inform periods of great transition. I am known to many as a rigorous modernist, and yet this vocabulary is always intuitively tempered by elements distilled from the penultimate moments of popular culture in combination with the most enduring traditions set forth by art—fine and not so fine. Invariably my modernism is transformed by my idiosyncrasies and by my enjoyment of both the tactile and tectonic into something quite unique, comfortable, and a physical testament to collabora-

tion between patron, designer, and craftsperson. My work is characterized by thoughtful architectural programs in which materials and details take their cues from the context of the project and the needs of the people who will ultimately inhabit it. An editor once referred to me not as an architect or as a designer but rather as a choreographer of spaces. Subsequently it has been my unspoken and humble pledge to honor this ideal, even if in my ambition, or in the harsh realities of the construction process, I fall short.

It was this very pledge that piloted my founding of Aero Studios during the recession era of Manhattan's Soho of the early nineties. It was essentially a Bauhaus philosophy that found a

Print Room, Mrs. John D. Rockefeller, Jr. apartment.

PREVIOUS SPREAD: *AUDAC exhibition, "Modern In-
dustrial and Decorative Art," The Brooklyn Museum,
Brooklyn, New York, June–September 1931. Donald
Deskey's guest room installation.*

new incarnation—a new application. At its very core was the belief that good design addresses the requirements of contemporary living with excellence in craft. These very same ideals and points of view were shared, and in many ways pioneered, by a visionary talent who also defied simple categorization. His clarity of purpose, although highly personalized, forged a design directive that would inspire leadership and optimism in what were otherwise the most troubled economic and social times our country had seen to date. I have always felt a kindred spirit in Donald Deskey, and I am just beginning to realize my debt and commitment to honoring his great legacy.

Donald Deskey's vast contributions to the worlds of visual merchandising, product design, industrial design, interior design, and architectural planning have never seemed more needed or relevant than at present. As barriers between fine and applied arts continue to erode, and as interior and architectural design too return to a typology that is more integrated, the disciplines more inextricably linked, Deskey once again serves as a model and an inspiration.

I have always considered design to be a language, a highly developed, often intuitive mode of communication, drawing upon a trove of culturally shared images and forms. I often judge the success of a design by its ability to communicate its ideas. Perhaps it is my own experience in retail design, packaging, and visual merchandising that allows me to identify with Deskey's earliest achievements and to appreciate his 1ac-

PHOTO: DONALD DESKEY COLLECTION, COOPER-HEWITT, NATIONAL DESIGN MUSEUM, SMITHSONIAN INSTITUTION.

Radio City Music Hall, 1932, Donald Deskey's first mezzanine lounge, mural depicting a map of the world by Witold Gordon.

complishments. Deskey's window designs for Saks Fifth Avenue not only showcase the particular product being offered for sale, but represent a stylistic point of view that positions the offering within a larger social context and therefore identifies the purchaser as a participant in a rarified discourse.

PHOTO: FRANÇOIS DISCHINGER.

William Sofield's Los Angeles residence with mural by Matthew Benedict. Sofield's employment of site-specific commissions has antecedents in Deskey's Stuart Davis commission for Radio City Music Hall.

It is precisely Deskey's refusal to distinguish between high and low art that I admire as most relevant today. Deskey draws upon the best that the industrial arts has to offer and applies this to the most luxe of residential commissions. Lamps intended for the refined chambers of the Rockefeller family are not conceived in ormolu and silk but rather glass and polished metal. These fixtures celebrate their utilitarian function and in doing so explore what it is possible to achieve with light.

New York penthouse designed by Studio Sofield. This apartment, once owned by Abby Rockefeller Milton, was originally designed by Deskey.

Conversely, Deskey continually draws upon the best of the fine arts and engenders these tenets to inform more banal commissions. In doing so, the ordinary routinely becomes extraordinary. Cubism, fauvism, constructivism, dadaism, and others all inform the patterns and surfaces of Deskey's interiors. Carpets, wallpapers, screens, and upholstery fabrics all bear witness to these noble antecedents. When the opportunity presented itself, commissions such as Stuart Davis's "Men without Women" for Radio City's gentlemen's lounge were integrated

The Bill Sofield for Baker signature collection features the Deskey-inspired pullman bed.

seamlessly with the decorative interiors. In doing so, Deskey crafts total environments incorporating the best and often the most poignant of what his culture has to offer.

The specific function of a given room is usually the point of origin for Deskey's design. The photography gallery in the Abbey Rockefeller apartment is a good example. Faced with a col-lection that exceeded the limitations of a modest room and that would only continue to grow, Deskey offered a clever and artful solution. He banded the room continuously with polished metal tracks to receive an infinitely recombinant display of photographs. This detailing then inspired the entire room, informing the doors and windows as well. I have had the good fortune of reworking this masterful apartment for a new owner. I have been careful to honor its visionary detailing.

If a major hallmark of Deskey's work is the incorporation of tectonic elements into residential design, an equally important inversion involves a residential treatment of public spaces. This is nowhere better evidenced than in his work at Radio City Music Hall. Here monumental spaces are made sumptuous and human by Deskey's intimate treatment. At the height of the Depression, when many large public spaces offered little more than the icy charms of a Nazi post office, Deskey's interiors inspired communal fantasy. Just as lavish stage shows helped people forget—if only momentarily—the harsh realities of Depression life, so too did the interiors offer the promise of residential splendor removed from the everyday. These were glimpses into a saturated and fanciful world, the world of the truly wealthy.

I find it fascinating that Donald Deskey brought industrial sobriety to the mega-wealthy and colorful grandeur to the middle classes. He functions as a cross-pollenator, an equalizer, bringing design elements—often out of context—to arenas where they may be seen and appreciated anew. I also subscribe to the notion that no design challenge is too big—or, for that matter, too small. I love the fact that the same man gave us the Clorox bottle, the Prell tube, and a highway lighting system, as well as the Abbey Rockefeller apartment and Radio City Music Hall. His sensibilities and energy seem uniquely suited to the situations and challenges we face today.

A double sink in a men's room designed by Philippe Starck.

John Stefanidis

~ on ~

PHILIPPE STARCK

Starck's style is defoliated but imaginative, and always provokes the senses.

Philippe Starck is a tease. I have never met him, so my impressions are gleaned from books, from the media, and from hotels he has designed that I have visited or where I have stayed. Starck is quintessentially French but belongs to a distinguished race of creative talent that straddles cultures and hence the world. Although a designer and not an artist (what either of these terms means in contemporary life becomes increasingly difficult to define), Starck is not unlike Marcel Duchamp; his influence transcends geographical boundaries and will endure, even though his reputation is mildly controver-sial. Philippe Starck has absorbed the surrealist movement; he is not afraid of kitsch; he seems to have looked at much modern art, and at the same time he is culturally infused by the very French, very chic talent of Christian Bérard; the ceramics of Jean Cocteau; and the furniture of Armand Albert Rateau, Eugene Printz, and Jean-Michel Frank. But Starck's greatest influence must be the towering giant of twentieth-century painting, Picasso—his visual jokes; teasing the eye; the unexpected and unconventional; the tension in composition; the abstract shapes of familiar objects; the juxtaposition of an eye; a handle; a profile with a full-on view of an eye—all of this is a familiar vernacular to this designer.

An artfully designed toilet designed by Philippe Starck.

Urination is a necessity shared by all, and very few places make it an exceptional event—the waterfall effect at the Royalton men's room in New York is an amusing accompaniment to a basic human need. Starck's gnome stools make you start; his chair for Kartell cocks a snook at furniture designers of the 1950s; his baby monitor is a jeweled pendant, his hair dryer a spaceship gadget; his juicer is a praying mantis in metal. His sense of scale is jokes that make you smile. One of my favorites is a container for parmesan in which the cheese grater fits into the lid—you are meant to grate the cheese into the container there and then. It is too cerebral since the parmesan grated in the morning for generous sprinkling on pasta will still be fresh enough to use on your potatoes au gratin in the evening—but enough of these frivolous complaints. The grater is made of cream matte plastic, its shape a truncated upside-down triangle with two cow horns protruding on either side. When you lift the lid, one of the horns is a spoon. It is a strangely satisfying object, easy to clean and for daily use, and it makes people laugh.

Philippe Starck is a pop designer (pop as in pop art = popular). Like anyone who is creative, he is full of contradictions, which often comes from having an impressive cultural repertoire. There are not many designers of the first rank with such a range of understanding of shape and colour, nor indeed painters or sculptors with as much wit who can tickle your eye and who are pleasing and alternative without being impractical. Starck straddles the worlds of luxury and inexpensive retail goods as a design colossus. He is to be found everywhere, but he is not easy to imitate.

Starck has a lifestyle which I have read is flamboyant—but is it? He has 11 different residences—a true cosmopolitan at ease in any world culture. And yet he has, on occasion, chosen to be photographed with his wife, the Eiffel tower in the background—a parochial Parisian, wearing a Davy Crockett hat to match his nascent beard perhaps. His wife Nomi smiles at him; good Hollywood teeth match red movie star lips. She is wearing a charity shop black-feathered hat of no distinction and a sleeveless black dress with a scooped neckline; on her bared flesh rests a row of large (but not very large) pearls, seemingly of good color (fake or real?). A bourgeois statement if ever there was one—but is it tongue-in-cheek, another tease?

Miami Beach in Florida has Art Deco skyscrapers built for New Yorkers in the 1920s and 1930s. These buildings are by no means great examples of pre-World War style, but they have escaped destruction by developers through the vicissitudes of the financial markets and that most fickle goddess—fashion. The beach is very wide and very long; above it is an ever changing skyline that is mostly blue with puffs of racing white clouds. On its esplanade are the tall,

PHOTO: TIM CLINCH.

Lime green cotton curtains with loose cotton net; fireplace inspired by the high Roman baroque period—Francesco Borromini and Donato Bramante. John Stefanidis outsized Rothschild chair inspired by French Art Deco.

seemingly endless pink, turquoise, yellow, white, and blue buildings. These exteriors make you joyful—less often the case when you are inside. The great and distinguished exception is Ian Schrager's collaboration with Philippe Starck at the Delano. The design is a stroke of genius. The hotel industry was forced to take notice, and hotel design has not been the same since. Up steep steps (made steeper or always this way?), a friendly welcome from white-clad attendants awaits you. The first part of the lobby strikes you as tall, the desk as long, and the concierge desk as small. Opposite and far away is a velvet sofa with an exaggeratedly high back. The chairs are all different—some contemporary, some vintage—and beyond are vast tall and wide cotton curtains billowing gently in the breeze. The message is immediate: we are in the tropics. In this wafting air, Dorothy Lamour might be sitting in the lobby, smiling, cross-legged and wearing a sarong. Is it palm trees you see beyond? Is this huge space really rather casually divided by the enormous and pleasing curtains? The answer is yes, and as you amble along forward, the light and the palms, the dark wooden walls and the furniture create an atmosphere that exudes a feeling of colonial ease.

Is all this an illusion? There are people sipping cocktails and chatting. There are some cool customers playing pool. At an angle to all this tranquility there is a marble ice-cracking bar, laden with seafood, where you savor your oysters, shrimp, or clams with chilled champagne or

PHOTO: TIM CLINCH.

Lobby to a bathroom in the tropics. John Stefanidis' "Malcontenta" chairs and tables. Shelves with gourds and a John Stefanidis–designed lantern.

white wine. Another step forward and there is a long, narrow bar, glowing pink, with a very long row of barstools. It looks crowded, but it is animated and fun—the smiling barkeepers work hard. You swizzle the stem of your glass and walk

past the indoor diners and out onto a terrace with huge, oversized pots (a Starck trademark), each containing a giant palm. At the bottom of the steps are more tall palms in rows that lead to a very large swimming pool designed to make you laugh out loud. It is very glamorous, but it is "taking the piss," as they say in London. It is a space given over to the senses. You relax on lounge chairs of all shapes and sizes; there is a round bar that serves poolside food; you can play chess with your feet in the water. Beyond is the beach— Miami Beach's pride—which Starck carefully includes in his decoration of the bedrooms above.

Back in the lobby, you rise in a stainless steel, no-frills elevator. As I recall, the hallways are long and painted white. The door to your room opens to more white. The floor is painted white; the large bed is covered in white linen. At eye level, as you enter, there is a witty Starck touch: a stainless steel support invisibly holding a large, luscious green apple for you to eat. It is both funny and appetizing. A shiny white cup-board incorporates a small, smart clock with an eminently visible face; the hi-fi, television, and a small refrigerator are also encased in white. These pieces are notoriously difficult to design and usually a sad apology in most hotel rooms, but Starck's cupboard is both well designed and well conceived.

In all this soothing whiteness there is an element that was part of the original building and unchangeable: a metal window, painted white, of course. Starck has changed it into a framed picture of the beach. It is a contemporary beach scene by Boudin—the sky is marine blue, speckled with racing clouds, white to match. The sand is also white and there are colored umbrellas and bronzed bodies power-walking or disporting themselves, playing beach tennis and volleyball. The picture has elegance, a live reminder of the spirit of place. It is the reason you are there, and the master designer, Philippe Starck, has made sure you will enjoy yourself. It is what he is all about.

OPPOSITE: *White stenciling on Havana brown walls in a bedroom. The Italian Empire parcel-gilt chairs are covered in white cotton as designed by John Stefanidis.* PHOTO: TIM CLINCH.

Carleton Varney

~ *on* ~

DOROTHY DRAPER

Her influence traveled around the world—from San Francisco to London to Petrópolis, Brazil—and she had a great influence on travel, from her designs for the Packard automobile to her creations for the C&O railroad cars to her interior designs for the Convair 880 jet craft. She created fabric designs, china patterns, even Christmas cards, and she was the first interior designer ever to license her name for home products and fashion as president of Dorothy Draper & Company, Inc.

After so many years of widespread imitation of her style, it is hard to reconstruct the impact

Dorothy Draper had on interior design. Hotels were revolutionized by her wizardry. Before she came along, lobbies all over the country looked pretty much the same: drab walls, Oriental-style rugs, potted palms, scratchy upholstery. In came Dorothy to "Draperize," a word coined to mean to give something "the look"—fresh, sparkling, and bright, as if a spring breeze were about to billow the curtains. Old, seedy, single-bed hotel rooms were transformed into magnificent places that looked like rooms in a great English country home. After World War II, Draper was riding high, throwing windows wide open and flooding rooms with sunshine, flinging color around like a mad painter. She bravely liberated the country from its self-imposed drabness.

When she did a job, she would first paint everything white—walls, woodwork, wainscoting, even whole paneled rooms. Then she might paint the ceiling pink, put down a green carpet, bring in a red chair and a black parson's table, and cover the sofa in chintz with big, blowsy, cabbage roses. The result was magic. Suffice it to say that having Dorothy Draper as your decorator was like having Yousuf Karsh take your picture or Luciano Pavarotti sing at your wedding. She was *it*, society's most prestigious imprimatur. Whether she designed a single room or a whole hotel, Dorothy Draper's name was the one you wanted to drop.

Dorothy Draper's career really took off in the 1920s when she was hired to decorate the Hampshire House in New York City. It was the first major job to display her inimitable style, and the largest decorating job awarded a woman at that time. The sliding glass shower doors she installed in the bathrooms were copied everywhere, as were the ornate baroque plaster moldings and wallpaper featuring great clusters of her beloved cabbage roses. She went on to Draperize the Essex House in New York City; the Quitandinha Hotel in Petrópolis, Brazil; the Arrowhead

PREVIOUS SPREAD: *Hampshire House (1937). Classic Dorothy Draper baroque look. Ceiling-height doors lacquered in blackberry with deeply cut white shaded moldings.*

Springs Hotel in California (a favorite watering spot for movie stars in its day); New York's Plaza Hotel; and the cafeteria of the city's Metropolitan Museum, one of her most successful jobs. There she installed white birdcage chandeliers, painted the walls aubergine, and gave the ceiling a canopy. It earned the nickname "the Dorotheum." Today, the Dorotheum has been repainted beige; the magic has been destroyed.

Did you ever wonder why woodwork from coast to coast is enameled white? Because Dorothy Draper decided it should be. When she couldn't find the furnishings she needed, she improvised. It was Dorothy Draper who first cut off the legs of oak tables and converted them into low coffee tables. She had cabinetmakers manufacture parson's tables before they were in style, and she installed big rhododendron hardware on chests to give them a little majesty. Many of her ceilings were painted a light sky blue, and all her jobs were awash with color and lots of it.

Dorothy Draper created magic, but the magic had a formula, one that few people understood. It was a combination of scale and color that made incongruous things work. The key was the unexpected note in the symphony that you're not ready for, the one that startles but never clashes. I understood the unexpected, the flair, and the willingness to be daring that either comes naturally or doesn't work at all. During those early years at Dorothy Draper and Company I immersed myself in her

The Garden Room at Hampshire House (as decorated by Dorothy Draper in 1937). Orange "trees," chintz covered chairs, black-and-white marble floor.

style, and then learned how to make it the basis for my own. I was in awe of Dorothy Draper then. We all were.

Mrs. Draper, as we called her, would often ask us which of two gift packages we would select: one wrapped in plain brown paper and twine or one wrapped in red-and-white striped paper and tied with a big green bow. Naturally everyone wanted the package à la Draper. She looked at rooms the way she talked about those packages, covering the walls with green-and-white striped paper, laying red carpeting on the floor, and covering furniture in splashes of red flowers, green leaves, and aqua bows on a white

The Greenbrier (as decorated by Dorothy Draper in 1948). Baroque overdoor plaster pediments, bishop sleeves draperies and valances—a Draper signature look.

background. To this lady, everything was a Christmas package. Timid she was not.

Her residential clients were the cream of international society, among them the Duke and Duchess of Windsor; Hope Hampton; and oleomargarine heir Micky Jelke, who later went to jail. A typical Draper Christmas at home featured a living room full of family as well as Who's Who. That living room, in the Carlyle Hotel, was one of the most magnificent I have ever seen. The high-ceilinged walls were painted eggplant with white trim. There were beautifully fringed beige draperies at the windows, a peacock blue satin sofa, white carpets on a dark-stained floor, and two bright red velvet chairs in front of the fireplace. Basil Rathbone sat in one of those chairs at every Christmas party and read Dickens's *A Christmas Carol* to the distinguished guests seated around him, champagne in hand.

Dorothy Draper influenced my life in many, many ways, and I have copied her traditions, adding my own touches since 1962. If that sounds like a long time to some (actually four decades), to me it is only a brief time—it seems like less than 20 minutes.

When I came to Dorothy Draper & Company I was in my early twenties—21, to be exact. The first projects I worked on included the lobby of a Park Avenue apartment building; the rooms and restaurant in a Washington, DC hotel; and the Sky Room restaurant of the Hotel Utah in Salt Lake City. The Draper office was an environment charged with diversity and energy, with Dorothy popping her head in and out of offices, overseeing everything, much as it is now with ongoing projects—The Greenbrier Hotel at White Sulphur Springs, West Virginia, being only one project that has been ongoing since my earliest days with the firm. I recall Dorothy working on her Westinghouse Dream Home for the New York World's Fair and updating her famous book, *Decorating Is Fun* (Art & Decoration Book Society, 1939). I recall Dorothy working on her fabric lines for F. Schumacher and

writing her syndicated column, "Ask Dorothy Draper," in which she gave advice to the many thousands of Americans who read her words religiously.

Dorothy Draper had entered the jet age when I appeared on the scene in the early 1960s. There were the interior designs of the Convair 880 for General Dynamics Corporation, some of which became part of the TWA fleet. There was the interior design of the public spaces of the International Hotel, then at what was then called Idlewild International Airport, and there were furniture lines for firms like Heritage. Dorothy was into design in a big way. She was multi-multi-multi, and that early awareness convinced me to open my own fabric house more than 25 years ago after having created fabric and wallpaper lines of my own for F. Schumacher; J. H. Thorp; Covington; Imperial; and my own fabric company, Carleton Varney by the Yard.

Dorothy was more than an industry leader: I credit her with creating an industry. Think of how many interior decorators there were in the early 1920s. Dorothy Draper always received raves for her work—even telegrams from Elsie de Wolfe, one of the few ladies who preceded Dorothy. Elsie and her lord sent a congratulatory telegram to Mrs. Draper on her accomplishments at the Arrowhead Springs Hotel in California in 1946.

Yes, Dorothy influenced me to be creative and expansive. I have decorated hotels, but also

Foyer in a suite in the Waldorf Towers (New York City), as decorated by Carleton Varney.

supermarkets, residences, cruise ships, show sets, apartments, and castles such as Dromoland Castle, Ashford Castle, and Adare Manor, all in Ireland. I have decorated for presidents and vice presidents of the United States such as Jimmy Carter, Walter Mondale, and Dan Quayle. I have followed Dorothy's lead by designing china for International China, and I also designed the official china for the residence of the vice president of the United States.

To continue the treatise about Dorothy Draper and how she influenced my life, I became a syndicated columnist in 1968 on Dorothy's death, when I took over writing the newspaper column, renamed "Your Family Decorator." I continue to write this column today. From designing hotel and restaurant uniforms as Dorothy did, I branched out and created a company called Carleton Varney Cruzanwear, where I designed tropical and resort wear—men's shirts, ladies' dresses, and pareos—and early in my career in the early 1970s I designed a line of men's hats from decorative fabrics for Hat Corporation of America.

I have always enjoyed writing, and among my 20-odd books are included a biography of my mentor, titled *The Draper Touch* (Prentice Hall, 1988), and two novels, *Kiss the Hibiscus Good Night* (Carol, 1992) and *The Decorator* (Shannongrove, 1999).

Dorothy Draper indeed has had a powerful influence on my life. I liked her color sense—a color sense few if any designers have been able

PHOTO: KIM SARGENT.

The Hibiscus Restaurant, Palm Beach Gardens, Florida.

to copy, or somehow to even figure out. How can you punctuate a light blue, white, green, and lavender scheme with vibrant red? And why, say some, would you want to? I believe, like Dorothy Draper, that to be a joyous place the world must be filled with clear, wonderful color . . . and I, like Dorothy, believe people can be blind to true color. I believe that you can take

A music room in a private residence in Savannah, Georgia, as decorated by Carleton Varney.

colors, patterns, and textures right out of nature and plant them inside, using far more than one print in a room. It all depends on scale. Does the flower garden exist with only one flower and one or two colors? Absolutely not!

It was always an adventure being with Dorothy—particularly on a train ride, be it to Philadelphia for a day or to the Greenbrier for a week's maintenance visit. Dorothy was a woman of a large frame, and she looked at times like a Roman gladiator as she wore a hat and, most often, white long gloves. Dorothy commanded attention by her stature, by her manner, and by her somewhat patrician voice. He social credentials were impeccable; she was a direct descendent of Oliver Wolcott, a signer of the

Declaration of Independence, and her grandfather had founded the New York enclave of Tuxedo Park. No wonder the tony hotels of the 1930s and 1940s wanted the touch of Mrs. George Draper (a.k.a. Dorothy Tuckerman Draper). There were the Carlyle, the Essex House, the Hampshire House of New York, the Mark Hopkins and the Fairmont of San Francisco. . . . In my time at Draper, I added to the Draper portfolio the Westbury Hotels of London, Brussels, San Francisco, Chicago, and New York; the Irish Castles of Dromoland, Ashford, and Adare; the Breakers; the Brazilian Court of Palm Beach; the Plaza of New York; the Copley Plaza of Boston; and the Arlington of Hot Springs, Arkansas.

The world has become smaller by way of communication and the Draper touch has been carried on from country to country since 1925. Dorothy Draper & Company is the oldest established and continually operating interior and industrial design firm in America.

Sister Parish's use of strong turquoise color sets off a collection of English eighteenth-century furniture sitting on a Sultanbad carpet with a Syrian mirror as a focal point.

Bunny Williams

— on —

SISTER PARISH

After getting my feet wet in New York working for a top English antique shop, I decided it was time to go to work for an interior designer, since this was the field I had originally wished to pursue as my career. There was only one person I really wanted to work for, so on an early spring day I knocked on the door of a small shop on 69th Street to inquire about a job. The three small rooms on the ground floor were the offices of Mrs. Henry Parish II, one of New York's top decorators, whom I had met during my time at Stair and Company and whose work I so admired, both from magazines and homes that I had seen. Luckily for me, Albert Hadley, her new associ-ate, needed a secretary and I was hired. Thus began a 22-year-long association with Mrs. Parish, known to everyone as Sister. Until the end of her life I always called her Mrs. Parish, mainly because I was brought up to use that form of address and because manners were very important to her.

For the first few years I had very little imme-diate contact with Mrs. Parish, as I was usually preparing estimates and placing orders, but I was lucky to be able to watch her hold court on 69th Street with the many fashionable clients that rang the bell and came in for a visit or to be shown something fabulous for their homes. Beautiful things came in and out of the offices,

Mrs. Parish's ability to mix colors and patterns was one of her great talents, as shown in her house in Maine.

luxurious fabrics were always being examined, and the constant activity was like great theater to a young girl from Virginia.

After a month or so I was asked to deliver some samples to a very elegant apartment on New York's Fifth Avenue, in one of the city's finest buildings. The clients were not at home, so the butler very kindly asked me if I would like to see the main rooms of the apartment. When I was shown into the drawing room, my heart almost stopped. Never in my life had I seen a

room like this. A fabulous art collection of Gauguins and Van Goghs hung on paneled walls lacquered the yellow ochre color of New York City taxicabs. Deep luxurious brown upholstered sofas were surrounded by beautiful French Regency chairs slipcovered in antique hand-blocked batik cotton. A huge coromandel screen wrapped the corners of the room. A tall gold French mirror hung over the mantel, almost touching the ceiling with a row of carved wooden camels marching across the mantel

This taxicab-yellow room drawing room was the first room that I saw upon my employment at Parish-Hadley. It opened my eyes to the excitement in interior design. Yellow living room paneling is based on the Hôtel Carnavalet. There are five different shades of yellow gloss.

shelf. But what I felt most about this truly elegant room was its sense of comfort. Though every piece was of the best quality, the arrangement of the furniture made this very large room seem intimate and inviting. There was great design to this room, but the design was not self-conscious. The room was designed to provide its occupants every comfort as well as to excite them. I knew that for me this was the soul of great decorating. I was so happy to be working for someone I hoped I would someday help to create rooms with this delicious atmosphere.

Mrs. Parish, who could not draw a plan to save her life, would walk into a room and immediately know where the furniture would go. It was amazing to watch her go into a room. She would walk around the space, study it for a short while, and then describe the floor plan: where

PHOTO: FRITZ VON DER SCHULENBURG. OWNED BY BWI.

A nineteenth-century burl maple four-poster bed is hung with crewel embroidery and sits on a Charles X French rug in Bunny Williams's bedroom in Connecticut.

the sofa would be placed, how a tall desk might go between the windows, or where a bookcase for the television would be perfect. She would describe seating groups that always allowed for at least six people to be comfortable talking together. She never used a tape measure, but just knew that the sofa would be seven feet long and the big side table against the wall would be six feet wide. When she later went shopping for the room, she was usually exactly right. When she spotted the perfect piece, it was sometimes within inches of fitting. We would always check the sizes with our tape measures and scale ruler, but she was seldom wrong. It seemed so effortless, but it came from having one of the most exacting eyes I have ever witnessed.

A paneled coffered ceiling in a house in Florida echoes the soft palette of the eighteenth-century French and Italian furniture in the living room designed by Bunny Williams.

A mixture of French and Italian furniture combined with a screen and table from the 1950s give a modern feel to traditional pieces.

What is the eye of a great decorator? The eye is a gift from God, like the natural ability of an athlete. If one has it, she would often say, it can be developed, but without it there is no chance. Her eye allowed her to mix pieces of large scale with small pieces. Her eye immediately saw the unusual shape of a chair leg that made it interesting, or the great color of a faded mahogany dining table that she might combine with a set of black lacquer chairs. For contrast, gilt sat next to polished mahogany, and old and faded painted pieces were combined with soft fruitwood. It was always about unique combinations of texture and color. There was always a sense of daring that created excitement.

Mrs. Parish was a traditionalist, but she was also an innovator, and she loved color. In the early 1960s tradition, decorating was about celadon green, creams, and gray blues, but the art scene was changing and Mrs. Parish thought nothing of painting a Fifth Avenue drawing room imperial yellow or a library in California a lapis blue lacquer. She would often begin a room with a great antique rug and then pick out the brightest colors for the walls or furniture. She would be very daring, but the color schemes would always be neutralized by using creams or beiges. We would work on a room's coloring by having many samples of paint and materials and arrange them together like a painting. I saw that a room of all intense color can become unsettling to be in, but a room with a balance of colors will never become tiring. Mrs. Parish always had a most unbelievable way of neutralizing a room by mixing old fabrics that were slightly faded with new fabrics in stronger colors. This always made the room feel evolved.

One of Mrs. Parish's most special talents was crafting rooms that seemed to have to have been done over a period of time. That came from the use of the old and new, both in furniture and fabrics, for the mixture of periods of furniture. There were no rules, just the natural

A great collection of English eighteenth-century furniture is scattered over a nineteenth-century French carpet in a soothing creamy-colored plaster room designed by Bunny Williams.

and uncanny ability to put a modern table next to a Hepplewhite chair or a contemporary painting above a Regency commode. There was always the ability to combine items in great style, such as a black lacquer commode with a basket. She always felt that a room of all very grand things needed something simple and natural; for example, she might have covered gold chairs in cotton fabric or placed painted tole cachepots on a polished mahogany cabinet. Charm was mixed with high style.

PHOTO: OBERTO GIGLI. OWNED BY BWI.

An incredible paneled room is filled with a combination of modern and antique furniture to complement a great art collection. Modern rugs tie the two furniture groups together designed by Bunny Williams.

Handicrafts were always a great love of Mrs. Parish's. She herself did charming decoupage pictures. Her love of patchwork quilts inspired her to commission the Freedom Quilting Bee in Alabama to produce a patchwork fabric that was used in a chic dining room in Georgetown. A sofa was covered in a large star-patterned quilt. A wing chair might be re-covered in a faded antique quilt in a paneled library. She loved working with weavers for special fabrics and rugs. She had her dear friend Alan Campbell, who was doing hand-waxed batiks for the fashion designer Halston's silk caftan, do bright pink batik fabric for the white French armchairs in her own living room. She was always exploring how to use artisans and craftspeople for her projects.

Almost as important as the creative stimulus I received over my long association with Mrs. Parish was the exposure to her fierce business integrity and discipline in organization that was aa important a part of my education as the designing. She taught us that we were in a service business and that service is what clients expect. A project must be finished, down to the tissue box covers and wastebaskets, and completed on time. Punch lists were constantly made on the minutest details. What good was a lamp without the perfect shade? Her fierce attention to detail was a great lesson. The organization of the office—the worksheets, the estimates, the billing—was just as important as the creative process, because without this no business will succeed. She also understood the power and necessity of publicity. She befriended the magazine editors and called them as soon as a project was completed and obtained permissions to have it photographed. She often worked on ideas for stories about design, and, because her story ideas were so creative, many were published over the years.

Mrs. Parish was a very complicated person. She had an amazing sense of humor and could keep one laughing for hours with her often exaggerated stories, but, at the same time, she could be excruciatingly cruel to her design staff, especially if she felt one was unprepared or if she sensed insecurity or weakness. Even this helped me see what I did not want to be. However, I had many, many wonderful times with her antique shopping along the way to anywhere, or sitting in her kitchen in Maine in our robes after a long day's work discussing our careers and life in general. Without her pearls and black dress in her khaki pants and L.L. Bean topsiders in her garden, surrounded by her family, whom she adored, she was another person. It was in watching her care for her own homes—always beautifully maintained—entertaining her friends in a glamorous but relaxed way that I realized more than anything that decorating was just as much about style and design and it was understanding how a house should work and function.

One other trait that Mrs. Parish had was always to choose the best people to have around her. I think the most important decision was choosing Albert Hadley as her partner. The genius of her work was a combination of the ideas of two of the most talented and inventive people I have ever known. Albert was an inspiration to all of us, including Mrs. Parish.

The most important part of having a mentor is using the experience as a footing and then going on to develop your own style and point of view. Even so, when I finish a project I do sometimes wonder what Mrs. Parish would think.

Ron Wilson

— on —

MICHAEL TAYLOR

One of my many clients is Cher. She and I began working together over 25 years ago, and to date I have completed 19 residences for her. In the mid-1980s, she asked me to design a home like nothing anyone had ever seen before. Of course this was a challenge, but because I knew her so well by that point, I knew that I had to perform her request. Fortunately for me, I saw a magazine article showing Michael Taylor and his work. His designs were so imaginative and so new that it gave me a direction for Cher's new project. The use of natural organic materials such as stone, hides, rock crystal objects, natural woods, rocks, textured walls, and overscaled uphol-

stered furniture was just one of the imaginative innovations of Michael Taylor.

Michael Taylor was a genius in his field. He originated a new design concept that the design world did not have before he came up with the idea. His genius that created this new design philosophy changed everybody's paradigm. His concept was elegantly casual, light, and airy, with overscaled furniture and many stone and other natural elements worked into a room's decoration. However, Mr. Taylor was not only brilliant at this new design concept. At the same time, he loved the finest of antique furniture. When he designed a project using antiques, his personal touch was clearly visible. This was achieved by his use of overscaled primary-colored fabrics placed on traditional furnishings, which created a stronger, contemporary, and more youthful statement than had been done in the past. It is impossible to replicate Mr. Taylor's genius; however, for me, he was a true inspiration because he expanded my idea and vision of design. Mr. Taylor finished his last project about 15 years ago—a home in Malibu that could only be described as a plain shoe box.

Cher was ready for an extremely contemporary design and called me immediately to see the house and go over the plans. Along with just finishing Cher's Italian villa, I had also recently completed two other residential projects plus a country club. I found myself very exhausted and did not think I could ever come up with a new idea for her or anyone else. When I met with her at that very plain house in Malibu, she wanted ideas on the spot. Frankly, at that moment, I did not have much hope for that house and had no idea what to say to her. My first reply was, "Why have you bought this terrible house?" Her

PREVIOUS SPREAD: *A Beverly Hills living room of contrast, both of color and texture. An ancient Roman fragment lies on top of the black granite hexagonal table that Taylor designed to fit with the oversized sofas covered in a burlap-weave, off-white silk, also designed by Taylor. Stone lighting fixtures lie on top of granite pedestals. Fittingly, a Banyan tree and a pen-and-ink drawing by Oscar Schlemmer lie between the bamboo shades.*

answer was that she knew that I could transform it into something very special. That really scared me. So I told her that it was a terrible house and I could not imagine how to make it better and that I needed time to think about it. Her answer was, "I don't think this is the time for you to work for me on this project." Her threat scared me so much that I was forced at that very moment to reach deeply within myself. Suddenly, I began to spout out a vision, the origin of which I did not know. But I did think of Michael Taylor's simplicity and elegant design. I suggested using stone floors throughout the entire house and glazing all the walls so they would appear to be stone. I used a natural nubby raw silk fabric on the overscaled furniture in the house. I also created my first draped bed, again using raw silk trappings. Every one of these ideas was something I had never done before. Cher's immediate reply was wonderful. "That's all I needed to do . . . scare you, and I knew you would perform miracles," she said. It was a miracle. I was given four awards for the Malibu project. Her reaction when she saw the finished product was flowing tears, along with a comment that she felt that the house wrapped its arms around her.

One of the reasons for my success is that I have never continued to decorate in just one way. Instead, I take chances and try to stay with the pace of new and exciting trends that I think have real merit and will withstand the test of time. But I do not use trends just for the sake of

In a Lake Tahoe living room, a twig construction sculpture by Charles Arnoldi and a pair of nineteenth-century Austrian metal-and-horn deer heads hang on walls of cedar siding. A raw rock coffee table lies in front of the sofa upholstered in hand-woven chenille. Taylor designed all of the upholstered furniture and benches.

A comfortable traditional Italian renaissance interior featuring fine eighteenth-century antiques and contemporary furniture of Wilson's design.

doing something trendy. Michael Taylor's look is a perfect example of separating the trendy from that which has real merit and staying power. I could tell that his designs, while wildly popular, were much more than just the latest fad in decorating. His talent was clear to me as well as to many others. As a designer, I think the real challenge is filtering the passing trends from the

truly new and innovative design ideas. I believe that this is the best way to stay current while still maintaining your own style and design ideas. A perfect example of my continually evolving designs is my recent redesign of a living room and master bedroom in a 1920s Beverly Hills Italian villa. The previous design, which I originally did over 20 years ago, was much more California casual and less interesting. The new incarnation of the living room has a huge seventeenth-century French limestone fireplace, dark hardwood floors, and eight-foot French doors that open onto a wonderful new terrace. The placement of the furniture is also a new design idea for me. I arranged a collection of antique armchairs, comfortable occasional chairs, a new sofa, and several interesting antique accent pieces into several small conversation areas within the living room in order to create intimacy and warmth within the very large room. In the past, I had used overscaled furniture in a more traditional living room layout (i.e., big sofa in the middle, two big chairs flanking the sofa, two lamps and two additional lounge chairs across from the sofa seating area).

In the master bedroom, I upholstered the

A master bedroom by Ron Wilson is filled with antiques. The walls are upholstered with suede, as are the bed trappings. The color scheme is peanut. The rug is an antique Moroccan.

PHOTO: JIM MCHUGH.

~ 201

A view from Cher's atrium looking toward the lounge. The fireplace has an Egyptian motif. The fabrics are leather and raw hand-painted silk.

walls in a peanut brown suede and created a simple but grand draped bed using the same material. I also used interesting antiques to add elegance and depth to the room, such as the eighteenth-century French chaise lounge and bibliothècque that conceals the 52-inch television the owner insisted on having in the bedroom. Along with these wonderful antiques and the drama of the upholstered wall and draped bed, I used a contemporary sofa, covered in a nubby raw silk, and built it into the corner of the sitting area.

In the early 1950s, Michael Taylor studied design in San Francisco at the Rudolph Schaeffer School of Design and later formed a partnership with Francis Mihailoff. He began his own company in 1956 and within four years opened his own shop in San Francisco. My professional education was very different from Taylor's. I barely had a high school degree and began my career on my own, struggling at first just to exist. I believe that the fear I had to survive helped to

In Cher's great room. Large overscaled furniture covered in raw hemp cloth and natural lamb. The walls are combed plaster.

A view from Cher's reception hall into the great room. The reception hall contains a pair of bronze oil-filled torchères that are early eighteenth century. All of the floors throughout the house are European stone.

PHOTO: MARY E. NICHOLS.

carve out the place I am in today. I learned as I went along and made mistakes in the process. However, my mind was like a sponge and I quickly learned right from wrong—what worked and what did not work. Fear acted as the cata-lyst for my success, but my interest in design and my ability to make my designs work for myself and my clients overcame any doubts I had.

I began by working with my older brother, who was a builder. He hired me as a superintendent. One year later, for no apparent reason, he asked me to furnish five model homes. I spent months at the library poring over *Architectural Digest* to see decorating ideas. It seemed to work for me. At the same time a decorator taught me scale and how to draw furniture floor plans. I eventually finished the model houses and they were a great success. I began to receive calls from people who had just purchased homes and had seen the models. They wanted the same draperies or carpets that I had put in the models. And some of the new owners even wanted me to furnish a room or two for them.

Just prior to this new beginning, Cher's mother purchased one of the homes that my brother had just finished building. This is how I first met Cher. She was only 13, and we became fast friends. Over the years, she told me that she had a crush on me and could not wait to watch me drive by her house. She has said that her crush lasted until she met Sonny. I've always been very flattered by her feelings toward me. When Sonny and Cher bought their first house, which was located in Bel Air and previously owned by Tony Curtis, I was the first to be called. It was my first of many exciting projects for them!

Vicente Wolf

~ on ~

DAVID HICKS

I n 1977, I was made aware of David Hicks. I was in the process of self-education on design and trying to make my learning curve a broader one. I had visited the standard traditional rooms of the Metropolitan and had looked through many issues of *Architectural Digest* and history books on design. I had been working in the Design and Decorative Building in New York and had visited all the Barbara Darcy rooms at Bloomingdales, and I had started to become aware of the lack of truly modern environments.

I had seen theme rooms, city apartments that looked like country French rooms, flocked wallpapers, and certainly classic contemporary environments created by Billy Baldwin that were done with restraint. But when I was given David Hicks's *Home Decoration* (World, 1972), I was jolted into really seeing my first truly modern lifestyle space. In his foreword, Hicks says, "Each designer in his lifetime really has one basic breakthrough, I think I have become known for my eclectic mixture of yesterday and today, placing a Louis XVI commode in a modern room—placing a modern picture in a period room. That, combined with an overwhelming interest in lighting, in colour and in pattern, is what I feel to be my contribution to interior dec-

A living room set on Jermyn Street; David Hicks's shop, 1978.

PREVIOUS SPREAD: *David Hicks's London living room, 1970, with painting by Ellsworth Kelly and cola-colored lacquered walls.*

A detail of Mrs. David Hicks's study at Britwell, 1966, room painted by Rex Whistler, 1937.

oration in the latter half of the twentieth-century." These were truly enlightening words to me, leading me to imagine the possibilities of creating a mixture of periods and forms but always having the focus of a contemporary room in mind—whether a modern office space or an eighteenth-century drawing room in Essex. The present was Hicks's arena. With his sense of sophistication and glib irreverence to the rules set down by some mystical designer in past times, new ground was broken.

It wasn't necessarily about altering the architecture but playing with it; about taking from the past but living with it today. It wasn't about furniture that had never been seen before but about *using* furniture like it had never been

Kitchen utilizing combination of traditional and contemporary forms. Custom-designed refectory table with chairs designed by Vicente Wolf.

seen before. Hicks discovered geometry in contemporary design in his wallpapers, fabrics, carpets, lighters, handbags, china, interiors of BMW cars, and even fashion items . . . virtually everything that hit the marketplace and the interior world with a bang. A simple design taken from an old tile bathroom floor revolutionized the interior design marketplace. To me, a young, struggling "learning to see" designer, this was awe inspiring. I had heard from Bob Patino, who worked in the Connaissance Showroom that carried David Hicks's fabrics and wallpaper in the United States, about this bigger-than-life persona that would sweep into the showroom and that you could surely tell he was British. I was intrigued, to say the least, and while I was starting to understand Hicks's design by dissecting and analyzing his work, I began to hear about his personal life. In short, I pulled all the elements of David Hicks apart.

Hicks's sophistication as a colorist reached a level never before walked on. He took the juxtaposition that he did so elegantly with furniture and achieved it with color for the dining room in his country house, where he brought together shocking pinks and rich burgundies that had never really been done in interiors and had only been approached in fashion by Schiaparelli or Charles James. He allowed you to travel the world to exotic places where color of great intensity is used every day, and again made it palatable for traditional spaces, taking furniture from the eighteenth and nineteenth centuries and setting it ablaze with a rainbow of rich tones and colors. Colors that gave a room depth and allowed you to see in a new, fresh way what up to that point had always been dealt with conventionally.

At the opposite end of the spectrum, he was adept with soft tones and washed-out pastel colors, bringing softness to bedrooms and living rooms. These colors glowed, but to me his most modern colorations were his range of neutrals: grays, blacks, whites, and taupes—colors that made the environment graphic, neutral but certainly modern. At the same time, the blending of textures gave all three styles of coloration depth, shimmer, and a richness that did not come from too much but always just enough.

I looked at his layout of furniture, a controlled and balanced plan that always had a surprise, and here is where I think his incredible merger of contemporary and traditional shined. He took all nineteenth-century furniture plans but gave them a sharp and modern sense. He had balance without being boring or redundant, and a sense of scale to the pieces that juxtapose straight lines with curves. His furniture plans have always been in the back of my mind each time I have started to design a room, having to create anew one more time but always still trying to maintain the past as my reference point. I have so many times looked through his books—which I know by memory—to try to catch a new nuance that I had perhaps not seen before. It is amazing to look at work that was done 40 years ago and yet is still so much in touch with the present, not growing old but still staying young. If we could only bottle that for our bodies, someone would make a fortune!

When I first started, I wanted every room and every plan to have never been seen before, to be groundbreaking and completely unique. I learned from David Hicks that that is not what always makes the best room. The kiss of death for a space is to be caught in time, to be seen as

A living room by Vicente Wolf, with an eclectic mix of furniture including a side table from Burma, a Chinese coffee table, and eighteenth-century Italian candlesticks (classic/traditional upholstery forms approached in a clean, modern way).

the equivalent of a poodle skirt in the realm of interior design. I did not know that this desire to be unique came with the territory of a beginner. Only time has taught me, when I look back at those rooms, that they did not stand the test of time. Only experience and hindsight have affirmed that the point of view of the master was clearly the way to go. A lot of Hicks's plans were innovative not because of what he changed but what he eliminated—a superfluous usage of furniture in spaces—just leaving it to the bare necessities.

The same thing he did with furniture plans he did with accessories—a sophisticated blending of items that always formed museum-like compositions. It didn't matter if one of the things in the composition was a plastic lighter and its only worth was the fact that the color worked with the rest of the composition. He took Deco objects, put them on lucite pedestals, and made them precious. He created tabletop landscapes, created a skyline with small details. It was an amazing formula he had; it could be done with dry twigs, eighteenth-century porcelain, or wonderful Oriental pieces. They all would dance to the tune; like a wizard, he would wave his wand and have them all stand at attention for him. Whether you saw them from above, straight on, or in profile, they all had great magic to them and yet such an extraordinary sense of spontaneity. It looks like he just plunked them down with no forethought. The more I write these words, the more I realize what an enormous influence he had on my career and

The juxtaposition of curved lines of the headboard against the square upholstery grid of the back wall gives this bedroom designed by Vicente Wolf a soft but still modern quality.

PHOTO: ©VICENTE WOLF.

PHOTO: ©VICENTE WOLF.

In this sitting room the play of scale involves a very high-backed sofa with loose back cushions juxtaposed with an eighteenth-century capital on a limestone pedestal, a silver chair used in nineteenth-century Indian weddings, and a carpet with an abstract design created by Vicente Wolf.

how no one is an island and no one creates in a vacuum.

My work speaks very clearly, but yet it seems that somehow, somewhere David Hicks's hand has, unknown to me, guided me. How unfortunate that I never met him—though he was prob-

ably better admired from afar. The last time I did a David Hicks room was about eight years ago. When I say I did a David Hicks room, I mean I was inspired by his furniture plan and coloration—funny enough for a small house in New Jersey. When I finished the project, I really felt

Tabletop landscapes created by Vicente Wolf bring a sense of scale and eclectic mix to both of these settings. In one, a photograph by James Hughes plays against a small Chinese writing tray and Tibetan nineteenth-century balls in a Swedish eighteenth-century decanter. In the second, a Chinese chest, a Thai fifteenth-century ball, a nineteenth-century Art Deco silver tray with objects from Japan and Burma, and Art Nouveau blown glass sit in front of a photograph by the Strand twins.

215

that I had cheated. It didn't look like any of his rooms, but to me it was clearly a David Hicks room. Maybe it was the furniture plan or the compositions in the space or the sense of color, but I felt surely that I should have shared my fee with him because he had worked on it has hard as I had. I don't know if it has to do with being older, but the more I have seen trends come and go, and styles become the rage, the more I am a true believer in the sense of spaces that have an elegant classic sense without compromising modern integrity. Of rooms that respect the past but never get overwhelmed by them. Of the sense of youth and vigor that modern spaces have. And those environments that have a blending of elements really stand the test of time.

DO'S AND DON'TS

— Pamela S. Banker —

Do start a collection. Be it blue glass, jade, bronzes, or butterflies, it will always be something to work with when designing and it will always be an interesting pursuit.

Do make use of wood on floors, paneled walls, countertops, and furniture. It brings warmth and texture to a room.

Do be constantly aware of scale and proportion as two of the most important elements of design. The scale of furniture must suit the proportion of a room. It's the golden rule of decorating.

Don't buy something simply because it's a bargain. It's worth waiting for things you really like.

Don't have too many lampshades in a room. Think about up lights and wall lights and be a little inventive about sources of light. A few lampshades are great in the right spots, but too many distract the eye from the design of the room.

Don't have too much clutter. Keep it simple.

— Mattia Bonetti —

Do

1. Do mix styles, materials, and colors freely.
2. Do follow your tastes and instincts.
3. Do treat yourself to pleasure.
4. Do dare to transgress the Don'ts.
5. Do dare not to follow the Do's!
6. Do ask Mr. Bonetti to redecorate your home.

Don't

1. Do not be afraid of what other people would say.
2. Do not become a fashion victim.
3. Do not be afraid to change.
4. Do not copy! Create!

— 217

— Thomas Britt —

1. Lighting is urgently important. If the budget allows, I like low-voltage recessed lighting, more often than not supplemented by lamps and sometimes up lights.

2. It is very important to create furniture groupings. I tend to like those that can interact with larger ones when the occasion calls for it. Always think in terms of large scale, whether for a grand space or the smallest space. This can be accentuated by smaller chairs or tables in juxtaposition with very large-scale sofas and chairs.

3. Have an open mind about color; use it daringly and in arresting combinations when the occasion calls for it.

4. Don't use heavy, thick rugs. I prefer thinner rugs, whether they are contemporaries, dhurries, Chinese, Bessarabians, or the occasional Aubusson.

5. If a room calls for an Aubusson, keep it played down—no curtains, or use simple architectural window treatments.

— Robert Couturier —

1. Distinguish between formal and informal spaces.

2. Never design a space from the exterior in, but rather begin from the floor plan and work outward. And always consider the basics specifically, such as how will it feel sitting in that room and how a person looks to others when walking through the space.

3. Texture is essential; there should be sensuality in the fabrics, whether an eighteenth-century Venetian brocade or a colonial needlepoint.

4. Simplicity of line—one that is finer and more elegant—must be critical to the entire design because a heightened simplicity will ultimately make the residents feel better. Cluttered spaces are depressing.

5. Copying line for line is really lying—a totally dishonest act. One should look for inspiration from the past but should have the modesty to recognize that there is very little that is new.

— Elissa Cullman —

Do

1. Begin each project with the living room carpet, the largest object in the house. Allow it to set the palette and personality of the decorative scheme, ensuring that there is a flow and continuity from room to room.

2. Create a layered lighting scheme utilizing a variety of sources including lamps, chandeliers, sconces, bookcase lights, and picture lights. Avoid down lights.

3. Design down to the most minute aspects of every project. From tabletops to custom linens and lampshades, God is in the details.

Don't

1. Don't create interiors that are slavish recreations of period rooms.

2. Avoid trends. Decorating costs too much today to end up being merely a fashion statement.

3. Try not to overdesign. Strive for tranquility and restfulness.

— Orlando Diaz-Azcuy —

1. Mundane things enliven luxurious decor.

2. People think I never use color, but it isn't true. Their eye just isn't trained, and they don't notice subtlety. Subdued colors are still colors. Some of our most exciting projects are true color inspiration. But I always look for the unusual shade, tone, or hue.

3. There's no cop-out in using pairs of things in a room. Matching chairs, sofas, lamps, or tables can bring discipline, strength, and balance to a scheme.

4. Simple interiors are the result of taking out, not putting in, a few things. A complex solution brought down to the minimal expression gets to the soul of the matter.

5. Contrast emphasizes the attributes of any interior.

6. Controlling and using light is the strongest element of design.

7. An interior without accessories is an interior without expression.

— Jamie Drake —

Do

1. Be bold in your convictions, especially when it comes to color. Nothing is more invigorating to a room than saturated colors in great juxtapositions, whether used lavishly or sparingly as accents.

2. Never forget to add a few off notes to keep a space interesting. A Tang horse in a Regency dining room or a sixties lamp in a room filled with FFF (fine French furniture) will add a dollop of dash.

Don't

1. Don't overlook the ceiling when scheming a room. A wash of color or shine brings the eye up and can highlight architectural detail, such as crown moldings.

2. Never light a room only from overhead. A variety of light sources is essential to creating an intriguing ambience.

3. Don't be afraid to be whimsical, even in a grand space.

— Arthur Dunnam —

1. Do look to the stylistic integrity of the structure and respond to it when formulating an approach.

2. Do consider the geographic setting of the project and endeavor to allow it to influence decisions and establish a tone.

3. Don't be afraid to evaluate the givens with a critical eye. Just because something is original doesn't necessarily make it right for the way we live today.

4. Do try to infuse spaces with unique elements of quality that give the rooms a true personality of their own, elevating them from the everyday.

5. Do strive for a relationship between client and designer that allows both parties to have pride of authorship in the finished product.

⏤ Ronald A. Grimaldi ⏤

Do

1. Do be able to make a decision—indecisiveness is lethal.
2. Do begin with one or two key elements and build from there (for example, existing carpet or color of the walls).
3. Do know your client's taste and lifestyle and cater to that style in the appropriate way.
4. Do remember that it's the client's house and not yours. Make the client happy without compromising your standards.
5. Do make decorating the fun experience it should be. Creating a good room is like getting dressed: earrings of the right proportion for your face and dress, shoes that coordinate with your handbag, and so on.

Don't

1. Don't become too serious with a room. If a piece has style and good proportions, it will stand own its own.
2. Don't worry too much over niggling details. Just get on with it!
3. Do not listen to your housekeeper's mother-in-law's opinion, or your painter's or your elevator man's. Trust yourself and your decorator.
4. Don't buy something for the time being. It's a waste of money. Leave the space empty until you find the right piece.
5. Don't follow trends too slavishly. They become trite and outdated all too soon.

⏤ Ashley and Allegra Hicks ⏤

Do

Look at sources other than shelter magazines for interior inspirations—altarpieces, not just *Architectural Digest*.

Be adventurous and enjoy yourself . . . at the end of the day, it's about pleasure!

Think about how you are going to live in the space: immaculate is rarely comfortable.

Include personal things so that a room talks about you—but in a subtle way.

Mix David Hicks carpets with Allegra Hicks fabrics and Ashley Hicks furniture—please!

Don't

Overaccessorize—you don't need to be your own stylist!

Have snapshots of every moment of your life framed, unless you are Bob Evans.

Follow fashion—nothing ages more quickly or wastes so much money and time.

Copy, unless you are really good at it.

Pay too much attention to lists of do's and don'ts.

━ Thomas Jayne ━

Do

1. Always remember what your most important goal for a room is. Is it a place to capture the sun, an office to conduct business, or maybe a cocoon to sleep in? Asking this question will make decorating choices easier to prioritize.

2. Make sure you plan for the major items you own first—your favorite work of art or a large desk. These are hard to casually fit in at a later date.

3. It is almost a truism, but rooms with beautiful proportions, even if they need to be smaller, are more beautiful and much easier to decorate. Try for tall ceilings in important rooms such as living rooms.

4. The decoration of each room in a house should have relationships to the others via color, style of furniture, art, and so on. This does not mean one should be a slave to one period of furniture or color scheme, just that a thread of common or repeating elements is employed to give a house a unified and satisfying atmosphere.

5. Try to have a custom or novel aspect in your decoration—an unusual color, a special molding, a custom piece of furniture. This is an allowance for a least a few things that are unique to you.

6. If you can afford it, always have a ballroom. It is a true luxury to always be prepared for a party.

Don't

1. Do not forget imagination, even if you have to work very hard at it. Obviously, lack of imagination leads to perfunctory decoration.

2. Do not compare the way you live to your perception of other people's lifestyles. This only leads to false competition and solutions that might not work for you.

3. Do not spend an entire budget for a room until you have every essential item planned for. You might end up with no money and an unusable room.

4. Unless they are truly beautiful, keep only a few inherited objects. This is all you need for sentiment.

5. Do not rely on one light source in a room. Not many of us look good in strong shadow—the light of a second opinion is always necessary.

6. Use black as a last resort—there is too much darkness in the world. Try dark grey or ebony brown. These colors are often more flattering and perform the role of black better.

━ Pauline C. Metcalf ━

Do

1. Always think about scale, proportion, and color.
2. Begin with a palette of colors from a painting, fabric, or rug.
3. Arrange seating for easy conversation.
4. Make light levels adjustable.
5. Have plenty of bookshelves.
6. Let a room tell about you!

Don't

1. Make everything match.
2. Have all the same style of furniture.
3. Make the room too perfect.
4. Forget the age of the occupants.
5. Be afraid of change.

⏤ Juan Pablo Molyneux ⏤

Do

- Recognize where your void is—and fill it in with knowledge.
- Have a point of view.
- Remember to be honest.
- Remember that, within a room, there are always four façades—the walls, floor, and ceiling—and give each of them equal attention.
- Remember that architecture and design tell a story—be sure you have one to tell.

Don't

- Approach the past as closed and far away.
- Be afraid of your setting—it's okay to modify a landscape or challenge it with an unexpected building.
- Give the same values to things. Make a hierarchy: the fireplace wall, for example, may have different weight in a room than an entrance.
- Repeat yourself.
- Stop studying, ever.

⏤ Juan Montoya ⏤

Do

1. Paint all the walls the same color in order to clarify the volume of the space.
2. My motto is, "The smaller the room, the larger the furniture." I feel that fewer pieces of greater scale in a room really make the room seem larger and more spacious. I hate rooms overstuffed with lots of small things.
3. Start the scheme of your room by first selecting and arranging the largest pieces. Afterward, follow with the smaller pieces and accessories.

Don't

1. Be selective; don't clutter a room with too many things.
2. Don't establish your furniture plan without analyzing your lighting as well.
3. Don't paint each wall a different color; it is confusing and doesn't allow for flexibility.

⏤ Roberto Peregalli ⏤

Do

1. Incorporate nostalgia: it is a reverie, a concept that means the dream we have about the past, filtered by memory.
2. Details make the difference between something that seems to have always been there and something that appears fake.
3. *Buttato lì* (literally, "thrown there") creates the atmosphere of something that appears casual, but is, on the contrary, absolutely thought out.

Don't

1. Do not pay attention to trends.
2. Do not overdesign.

⌒ Suzanne Rheinstein ⌒

Do

Give in to eighteenth-century painted chairs. They move easily and look divine.

Buy fewer but better pieces of furniture and art.

Mix comfort and chic.

Remember rock crystal, silver, and old mirrors are very glamorous.

Bring out too many candles at night—indoors, of course, and outdoors in lanterns to conjure up the best mood.

Don't

Forget to keep most things in the closet and not on your tables and chests.

Think beautifully blocked chintz is passé just because it was once everywhere.

Feel you have to have flowers in a garden. Clipped green architectural gardens are enchanting.

Stop trying to edit, edit, edit.

Forget that Elsie's famous pillow said, "There are no pockets in a shroud."

⌒ Betty Sherrill ⌒

Betty Sherrill does not believe in do's and don'ts.

⌒ Marjorie Shushan ⌒

Do

Group a collection together—there is strength in numbers.

Choose a color and use it for fabrics, walls, and accessories for a clean, luxurious look.

Go with your intuition but keep an open mind. There is more than one solution to a challenge.

Invest in the shell of the interior. It is important that the space have good bones and symmetry.

Often your first ideas are your best.

Don't

Don't use furniture of only one particular style or period. Be imaginative and eclectic.

Don't make abrupt changes in colors when moving from room to room.

When dealing with a low ceiling, do not mount curtains at the top of the window; take them to the ceiling. It will give the room height.

Don't use small furniture because a room is small. Anchor the room with a few well-proportioned pieces.

Don't ignore location and architecture when doing the furnishings.

⚊ William Sofield ⚊

Do

Let the design and detailing of a room be derived directly from its function.

Understand what is most unique about a space and celebrate it.

Have knowledge of what is happening in the fine arts and incorporate the best into the project.

Have knowledge of what developments are happening in the technical arts and incorporate the best of these materials and inventions into the project.

Create an environment that is a joy to use and that will improve with age.

Don't

Ignore the basic spirit of the space in which you are working.

Determine a style or vocabulary before you consider the precise use of the space.

Ignore how light moves through a space.

Forget that you will not live there, your client will, and the space must work for him or her.

⚊ John Stefanidis ⚊

Do

Use your imagination.

Consult experts.

Don't

Look at books to see what you like. Prepare a dossier and confide your clearly stated ambitions to those who can execute what your heart desires.

Don'ts are unacceptable formulas.

⚊ Carleton Varney ⚊

Do

1. Painted ceilings are favorites of mine. I often paint ceilings Jefferson blue, to match the sky, and I like pale pink and soft yellow too. Ceiling color does not have to match wall color. I like ceiling trim to be painted white semigloss enamel.
2. Chandelier chains should be covered with a sleeve—oftentimes velvet—or with some bag-style decoration. I often use white silk to cover unsightly metal or brass chains, particularly in handsome period-style rooms.
3. Every room needs a touch of black, be it a Chinese lacquer coffee table, a picture frame, a porcelain vase lamp, or a needlepoint seat on a special pull-up chair. Black tends to give gravity to a room.
4. I like to see wing chairs used in pairs, and never

or rarely singly. I call the wing chair the lonely chair, and I like to see it always accompanied by a mate.

Don't

1. Overdraped and festooned window treatments are not favorites of mine. Sometimes the simpler treatments work best, and they are much easier to care for.
2. I never use floral prints where the flowers in the print look dead. In other words, roses that are gray or beige are best left on the racks in the fabric showroom as far as I am concerned. If a print, particularly a flowering print, looks dull, it is not in my decorating thinking.

3. I very rarely use matching night tables (except in my hotel work, where maintenance is a factor). I like night tables that have ample surface, and sometimes drawers and pull-out slides. I often use a desk or a round skirted table at bedside.
4. Some say that small rooms should be painted, or their walls covered, with light colors to make them look bigger. I disagree. No matter how light you paint a wall, or how much mirror you use on a wall, small rooms always have the same amount of floor surface. I generally use dark colors in rooms that are small to give a cozy feeling to the space—and there is always a light in the corner (preferably a lamp).

⁓ Bunny Williams ⁓

Do

- Educate yourself in the decorative and fine arts. Knowledge is essential.
- Be daring. Always try one new idea.
- Try to remove one thing a month from a cluttered room.
- Add one thing a month to a minimalist interior.
- Mix the past with the present.

Don't

- Don't use every idea you ever had in a room.
- Don't overdo—it will become tiring.
- Don't be afraid to try a new idea.
- Don't use all things of the same style and quality in a room—opposites attract.

⁓ Ron Wilson ⁓

Do

1. Do always use a professional designer.
2. Do rearrange hotel room furniture to suit your tastes.
3. When working on a budget, keep things simple—don't get too complicated.

Don't

4. Don't blindly follow the latest trends.
5. Don't be afraid of imaginative ideas.
6. Don't ask for too many people's design opinions.
7. Don't use wall-to-wall shag carpeting.
8. Don't use home craft design techniques that you see on television—if it looks too good to be true, it probably is.

— Vicente Wolf —

Do

1. Get good quality upholstery; it will stand the test of time.
2. Experiment with countries, periods, and cultures when selecting furniture.
3. Display your collections together. It makes a much stronger statement than dispersing the pieces around the room.
4. Use picture rails or simply prop art against the wall; then you can move pictures around and see them in a different light. When a picture is in one place for too long, you stop looking at it.
5. Break the rules.

Don't

1. Don't ever feel that lighting is not important; it creates the mood. Think of an empty stage with good lighting.
2. Don't get reproductions; try to find something authentic. It doesn't have to be museum quality.
3. Don't pick one hue for a room and try to match everything too closely. Choosing two or three shades of the same color running through walls, carpentry, and upholstery gives a room some depth.
4. I would never use silk or dried flowers. Fresh flowers embody a moment in time; the fact that they are ephemeral is part of their beauty.

BIOGRAPHIES AND CONTACT INFORMATION

—

KALEF ALATON (1940–1989) studied painting and sculpture in Istanbul and Paris with the early goal of becoming an artist. At 16 he turned his talents to interior design, studying with Russian designer Oscar Mourinsky. In that same year, he completed his first project—a house for his father. In 1968 he came to the United States to work for a large design firm. He started his own company in 1973. Based in Los Angeles, he worked not only in the United States but internationally as well. Kalef has been published numerous times in *Architectural Digest* and was made a member of the Interior Design Hall of Fame in 1988.

BILLY BALDWIN (1903–1983), a native of Roland Park, Maryland, went to New York City to work as an assistant to Ruby Ross Wood (1880–1950), who was Elsie de Wolfe's former assistant (actually her ghostwriter for *The House in Good Taste*) and who eventually became a major competitor. Baldwin opened his own firm (Baldwin & Martin) in 1952. Clients included Jackie Kennedy, the Lawrences, the Paleys, and Diana Vreeland. Baldwin authored three books during his career.

PAMELA S. BANKER, a native New Yorker, had her own decorating firm for more than 20 years before joining McMillen, Inc. in 1990 as a vice president. In 1995 she joined Parish-Hadley Associates, Inc. as a vice president; and in 1999 she launched Pamela Banker Associates, an interior design and decoration firm with offices in midtown Manhattan. Throughout her career, Pamela Banker has designed interiors in this country and abroad for residential clients, private clubs, and corporate clients.

Banker's work has been featured in *Architectural Digest, House & Garden,* and British *House & Garden.* Her house on Long Island was included in the book *Weekend Houses* by Penelope Rowlands.

Pamela Banker
136 East 57th Street
New York, NY 10022
Tel: 212-308-5030/5304
e-mail: psb@pamelabanker.com

GERMAIN BOFFRAND (1667–1754) was a distinguished French architect and designer of private palaces and hôtels particuliers for the aristocracy during the reign of Louis XV, as well as engineer of the

Pont de Joigny and Pont de Villeneuve-sur-Yonne. Other works include Amelot; Château de Lunéville, Lorena; Palace of the Malgrange, Nancy; Palace Ducal, Nancy; and Hall of the Princesse of the Hôtel de Soubise (considered to be one of the finest representative examples of French Rococo interiors. Boffrand was the author of *Livre d'architecture contenant them principles généraux de cet art* (1745).

MATTIA BONETTI was born in Lugano, Switzerland, in 1952. After pursuing artistic studies, he established himself in Paris in 1973, where he designed for the textile industry and worked as an artist/photographer. In 1979 he became a designer/decorator and has since created numerous collections of furniture and objects, including unique pieces, limited series, and items industrially produced for wide distribution.

Bonetti has designed numerous interiors for private residences in France and abroad. He has imposed a design that freely mixes the accoutrements of international decorative arts with the most modern lines, thus giving birth to a very personal new style.

Mattia Bonetti
10, Rue Rochebrune
75011 Paris, France
Tel: 33-01-48-05-61-21
Fax: 33-01-48-05-61-29

STÉPHANE BOUDIN (1888–1967), the legendary French designer, was the son of a passementerie maker; in 1923 he went to work for the House of Jansen and eventually became its president. With a commission from Elsie de Wolfe, Lady Mendel, to design a pavilion at Versailles, he became the "decorator's decorator." Boudin designed the homes of the very rich—the duke and duchess of Windsor, the Paleys, Lady Baillie of Leeds Castle, the Guinesses, the Wrightsmans, the Guests, H. J. Heinz, Stavros Niarchos, and Agnelli—and created for them a stage set on which their desires and fantasies could be fulfilled. In 1961 a committee was formed

with Henry F. du Pont to design several rooms at the White House under First Lady Jacqueline Kennedy.

THOMAS BRITT, a native of Kansas City, Missouri, received his design training at Parsons School of Design both in New York and in the European programs of the school. He also holds a bachelor of science degree from New York University. After graduation in 1959, he was associated with interior designer John Gerald for five years before starting his own design firm in 1964. In addition to his design activities, he was associated for five years with famed South American designer William Piedrahita of Bogotá in a furniture design business with outlets in New York, Texas, California, and Bogotá.

His clients include Her Highness the Raj Mata of Jaipur, Princess Priya Ransit of Thailand, Prince Rani Priya of Jaipur, U.S. Ambassador to the court of St. James Charles Price and Mrs. Price, Count and Countess John Forgach, The Jorge Larrcas of Mexico City, the Nicholas Zapatas of Mexico City and New York, Frederick Woolworth, Clark Swansons, Mr. and Mrs. Frank Paxton, Mr. and Mrs. Thomas Jefferson Wood, Sidney Richard, the Seymour Milsteins, Mr. and Mrs. Peter Soloman, and Mrs. Barbara Schreck of Grosse Point.

Britt's career is listed in *Who's Who* and *Who's Who in the World,* and he has been published in *House & Garden, Architectural Digest, House Beautiful,* and *Town & Country* as well as numerous European publications.

Thomas Britt
136 East 57th Street
New York, NY 10022
Tel: 212-752-9870
Fax: 212-888-8735

ELEANOR BROWN (1890–1990) was born in St. Louis, Missouri. She was a leading interior decorator and the founder of the decorating firm McMillen, Inc. in 1924 after she completed professional training at the Parsons School of Design in New York and Paris. Hers was one of the first professional full-service decorating establishments in the United States. Her firm first acquired an international reputation by designing the interiors of apartments, country estates, private clubs, and even yachts and airplanes of prominent families in the United States and abroad. In 1952, Brown was made a chevalier of the Légion d'honneur by the French government. In 1953, she was awarded the Parsons Medal for distinguished achievement in design. She was a former chairman of the board of Parsons School of Design and a former board member of the Newport Historical Society and the English Speaking Union.

In 1963, Brown was selected by Jacqueline Kennedy to decorate portions of Blair House, the U.S. Government's Washington guest house for foreign dignitaries. During the Johnson administration, her firm also decorated the president's private quarters in the White House. In the 1960s, Brown expanded the firm's activities into the commercial world by designing offices for such companies as Solomon Brothers, Morgan Stanley, Mobil Oil, St. Regis Paper, and Chemical Bank. In 1982, Viking Press published a retrospective of the firm's work, *Sixty Years of Interior Design: The World of McMillen.*

ROBERT COUTURIER is a noted French architect and designer based both in New York and Paris. His distinctive creative sense, matched by his intense knowledge of the decorative arts, has enabled him to make *Architectural Digest's* Top 100 Designers list.

Couturier grew up in a Hector Guimard–designed hotel particulier situated in the stylish 16th arrondishment. An endless round of visits to such important residences as the Chateau de Groussay filled his early years. His knowledge of the decorative arts is unparalleled. He studied at the École Camondo and worked under Adam Tihany on a series of residences for Dino De Laurentis and the actress Silvana Mangano. In 1986 he founded his firm with commissions from Sutton Place maisonettes, Aspen ski lodges, an eighteenth-century chateau, and the late Sir James Goldsmith's 60,000-square-foot palace in Careyes, Mexico.

Robert Couturier
69 Mercer Street
New York, NY 10012
Tel: 212-463-7177
e-mail: aproject@robertcouturier.com

ELISSA CULLMAN and the late Hedi Kravis founded Cullman & Kravis, Inc. in 1984. "Interior decorators for collectors of fine art and antiques," Cullman & Kravis is known for its broad versatility of design with special concentration on the American and English styles. The firm's clients have included the CEOs of Miramax, Philip Morris, Paramount Communications, Salomon Brothers, New Corporation of American, Goldman Sachs, DDB Needham, The Blackstone Group, and corporations such as Seagram's, Countess Mara Esmark, The Regency Hotel, and Claridge's in London.

Cullman, a Phi Beta Kappa, magna cum laude graduate of Barnard College, was a guest curator at the Museum of American Folk Art and is coauthor of *Small Folk: A Celebration of Childhood in America* (New York: Dutton, 1980). She has been a member of the Museum of Modern Art's Contemporary Council since 1973, and a board member of the Film Society of Lincoln Center, Inc. since 1974. She was a trustee of Barnard College from 1989 to 1996, and joined the board of the Brooklyn Museum of Art in the fall of 1998. She also sits on the board of Friends of Florence, a nonprofit organization dedicated to preserving the arts of Florence.

Cullman was included in the *Architectural Digest* 100 in January 2000 and 2002.

Elissa Cullman
Cullman & Kravis, Inc.
790 Madison Avenue
New York, NY 10021
Tel: 212-249-3874
Fax: 212-249-3881

ROSE CUMMING (1887–1968) started her firm in 1917. She was one of the first women to create the interior decorating profession as we know it today.

Armed with nothing more than good breeding and good taste, she set up shop on New York's Madison Avenue and created what has become one of the legendary shops in New York. She was one of the first to import beautiful chintzes and silks from Paris and London, which were especially colored to her unique tastes and which are still an integral part of our collection today.

DONALD DESKEY (1894–1989) was a pioneer in furniture, interior, graphic, and industrial design. He helped to establish the style that became known as streamlined modern. He created objects as diverse as pianos, clocks, radios, slot machines, and industrial laminates. Born in Minnesota, he studied architecture at the University of California as well as at the Mark Hopkins Art School, the Art Institute of Chicago, and the Grande Chaumière in Paris. In 1925, he moved from Paris to New York to establish with Phillip Vollmer Deskey-Vollmer, a furniture and textile design company.

High-profile commissions were John D. Rockefeller's Manhattan apartment and the interiors of Radio City Music Hall (1932–1933). Deskey worked with chrome, aluminum, bakelite, and innovative materials. He exhibited at the Paris Expo in 1937, the Metropolitan Museum of Art, the Brooklyn Museum, the Detroit Institute of Art, the Chicago World's Fair in 1933, the New York World's Fair in 1939, and the Museum of Modern Art.

In the 1940s, Deskey worked as a graphic designer; his designs for Tide laundry detergent, Prell shampoo, Crest toothpaste, and other packaged goods are now firmly embedded in American consumer culture.

ELSIE DE WOLFE (1865–1950), a shrewd businesswoman and a pioneer in interior design, established her career when she designed the Colony Club in New York City in 1907. Elsie received enormous commissions for counseling Henry Clay Frick (the most important art collector at that time) on his purchases of fine French furniture. Other clients were the William Crockers, the Ogden Armours, the Weyerhaeusers, and Ethel Barrymore. Elsie authored an autobiography entitled *After All* (Harper, 1935). She was decorated with the Croix de Guerre and the Légion d'honneur by the French government for her war work (1914–1918).

ORLANDO DIAZ-AZCUY is a secret romantic. While his interiors tend to be minimally detailed, there is always a touch of va-va-voom. Masa's restaurant has its red lacquered armoire. Serene living rooms are jolted with lavender silk velvets, acid green silks, gilded Fortuny fabrics and a retinue of contemporary paintings and sculptures. "I am always battling design conservatism and clients' perpetual longing for the familiar." Diaz-Azcuy says. "I like to stretch my clients as far as possible." Cuban-born Diaz-Azcuy is a designer's designer, a 62-year-old grand master who is skilled at doing it all: commercial and residential work, gala decor, landscape architecture, and furniture design. His clients include social trendsetters and high-tech billionaires. Design projects include the spa at Hong Kong's Peninsula hotel, a chic lounge at San Francisco's War Memorial Opera House, law offices in London, athletic clubs in Northern California, a Los Angeles cancer center, and an ever expanding line of furniture under his name for McGuire. He is the man in the legendary starched white lab coat.

Orlando Diaz-Azcuy Designs
Tel: 415-362-4500—San Francisco
Tel: 212-223-7767—New York City
e-mail: oda@odadesigns.com

JOHN DICKINSON (1920–1982), a California designer, is one of the most admired, inspired, and emulated figures in the world of decorating and furniture design. Born in Berkeley, the designer eschewed formal design education, and yet his designs for hotels, residences, restaurants, corporate headquarters, and many other commissions around the country always show his deep understanding and knowledge of design history. His signatures are an extraordinary refinement, a superb sense of proportion, and a rigorous editing process.

Dickinson's career was all too brief—a mere two decades—but even before his death in 1982, he quickly became a cult figure in design. His sculptural, beautifully proportioned, and highly original decor is admired today around the world. His iconic and now rare plaster and metal tables and other custom designs are among the most sought after among antiquaries and at auction, and his legacy seems stronger than ever.

JAMIE DRAKE, considered a trendsetter in the field, is one of today's most celebrated interior designers. He is legendary for creating uncommonly glamorous high-end residences with that "Jamie Drake flair." Borrowing elements from fashion, cinema, live theatre, and music, Drake's interiors spark visual interest and intrigue.

Drake Design Associates' client roster, over the last 25 years, includes high-profile commissions for Madonna and numerous projects for New York City mayor Michael R. Bloomberg. Drake is honored to have just completed the restoration and renovation of Gracie Mansion, as well as various rooms at New York's City Hall. Drake's work has been featured in many publications including *House Beautiful, Elle Decor, House & Garden, New York,* and *The New York Times.*

Jamie Drake/Drake Design Associates
315 East 62nd Street
New York, NY 10021
Tel: 212-754-3099
Fax: 212-754-4389
Web site: www.drakedesignassociates.com
e-mail: jamiedrake@drakedesignassociates.com

DOROTHY DRAPER (1889–1969) was the prima donna of the decorating business in her day; one of her many dictums was, "If it looks right, it is right." She was born in 1889 in Tuxedo Park, New York. Incredibly versatile, she not only decorated residences and hotels but also packaging (Dorothy Gray cosmetics), air-planes (TWA interiors in red/white and black), and even a Dodge pickup truck for a Chrysler show in the 1950s (in pink and white polka dots). She gave decorating advice to millions in *Good Housekeeping* and designed fabrics and furniture. She developed the concept of design beyond the arrangement of furniture and accessories and broke away from the historical period room style that dominated the work of her predecessors and contemporaries. She invented modern baroque, a style that had particular application to large public spaces and modern architecture. Her use of black-and-white checkered floors; elaborate plaster decorations of ferns, leaves, or shells; mirrored door frames and columns; baroque overdoor plaster pediments; sugar frosting candelabra chandeliers; and dazzling color everywhere was prominent in the countless hotels that she decorated: the Fairmont and Mark Hopkins (San Francisco); the Quitandinha (Brazil); the Camellia House (Drake Hotel—Chicago); the Greenbrier (West Virginia); the Arrowhead Springs (California); the Plaza (New York); and "the Dorotheum" (Metropolitan Museum, New York). Her famous touch was a merger of her unique color sense—everything was awash with color combinations never before attempted, plus her two favorites, dull white and shiny black—and a few good pieces. This powerful and magical formula was called the Draper touch.

To Dorothy, public space represented a place for people to come and feel elevated in the presence of great beauty, where the senses could look and feel and absorb the meaning of a quality life. That any of her work remains years after her death in 1969 speaks volumes about her talent. Her touch has survived in a time that does not value the past. She was truly the last grande dame.

ARTHUR DUNNAM was born in Shreveport, Louisiana, in 1958. After graduation from Washington and Lee University and a summer job as a surveyor for the Virginia Historic Landmarks Commission, Dunnam attended the Graduate Design Program at Pratt Institute. Concurrently he began a career in the office of Arthur Smith, partner of Billy Baldwin.

In 1986, Dunnam joined Jed Johnson & Associates. As the design director since 1997, his projects display an array of styles, from a Manhattan penthouse that embodies its occupants' appreciation for period English and Continental furnishings accented with twentieth-century art (*Architectural Digest*, February 1998) to a Stanford White–style mansion infused with the owner's love of crafts (*House & Garden*, August 2001) to two recently completed period restorations in New York's noted Dakota and his own relaxed seaside cottage (*Architectural Digest*, September 1999). All of Arthur Dunnam's work exhibits meticulous attention to detail and respect for the architectural integrity of the structure, sensitivity to the setting, and, most important, understanding of the lifestyles and wishes of his clients. His work has appeared in numerous design periodicals and will soon appear in Stephanie Hoppen's curtain book.

Arthur Dunnam
Jed Johnson & Associates
211 West 61st Street
New York, NY 10023
Tel: 212-489-7840

HENRY FRANCIS du PONT (1880–1969), a scion of Delaware's industrialist du Pont family, was born at the family estate known as Winterthur and, in his own words, "always loved everything connected with it." After assuming responsibility for the estate upon his father's election to the United State Senate in 1906, du Pont began to develop and improve its garden areas. Within a decade, du Pont began to expand his family home to accommodate his burgeoning collection of decorative arts objects and historic architectural elements, doubling the size of the existing house.

Throughout the next two decades, du Pont and his family lived in a museum in progress. In 1951 du Pont turned his house over to the Winterthur Corporation, a nonprofit educational institution. The Winterthur Museum opened to the public. In 1961 the first lady, Jacqueline Kennedy, visited Winterthur and invited du Pont to head the Fine Arts Committee, which oversaw the restoration of the White House. Until his death in 1969, du Pont divided his time among his homes at Winterthur; Southampton, Long Island; Boca Grande, Florida; and an apartment in New York City.

FRANCES ELKINS (1888–1953) is known for her ability to mix American traditional styles with French and English antiques. Born in Milwaukee, Wisconsin, the sister of the well-known Beaux-Arts–trained architect David Adler received most of her design training through travels with her brother in Europe. She moved to California in 1918, bringing a taste for haute couture and Art Moderne. By 1927 she opened an office in Monterey, and decorated numerous homes San Francisco Bay Area. During the 1920s and 1930s she collaborated with her brother on elegant houses in Chicago. She soon became recognized for her ability to combine European antiques with contemporary arts and crafts. She was among the first to introduce the work of Jean-Michel Frank and Diego Giacometti to this country. Her outsize scale and daring juxtapositions were influential on other interior designers, including Billy Baldwin and Michael Taylor.

Later she became known for an eclecticism that mixed pieces by California craftspeople, along with Mexican influences, but she never allowed a single theme to overwhelm her composition. Elkins's talents enabled her to create a personal anthology of taste and design that was freer than those of her contemporaries who relied on the stricter interpretations of historical styles. This eclecticism became an important influence on decorating in the later decades of the twentieth century.

JEAN-MICHEL FRANK (1895–1941) was perhaps the most influential designer and decorator of the Parisian haute monde of the 1930s and 1940s. He designed complete and total interiors—room architecture as well as furniture. His style was based on refined simplicity and on the quality and rarity of materials used.

JACQUES-ANGE GABRIEL (1698–1782) is considered to be one of the most distinguished French architects of his century. He was trained by his father, Jacques Gabriel V, and by Robert de Cotte. In 1742 he succeeded his father as the premier architect for Louis XV at Versailles.

Gabriel's masterpieces are the Place Louis XV (the present-day Place de la Concorde, which includes the Ministère de la Marine, the Automobile Clube, and the Hôtel Crillon); the École Militaire; the Petit Trianon (designed for Mme. de Pompadour; later given by Louis XVI to Marie Antoinette); and the Opéra Royal (opened for the wedding of the future King Louis XVI and the Austrian archduchess Marie Antoinette).

EILEEN GRAY (1879–1976), born in Ireland, attended the Slade School of Art in London, then moved to Paris in 1902 to create furniture and accessory designs. She established herself as one of the leading designers of lacquered screens and decorative panels.

She designed two houses in the Alpes Maritimes: from 1927 to 1929 she built her famous house in Roquebrune called "E1027" and the other house, at Castellar (1923–1924). Both houses are considered to be among the purest examples of domestic architecture and interior design of the period. In 1972, she was appointed a Royal Designer to Industry by the Royal Society of Art, London. The Museum of Modern Art in New York holds the E1027 adjustable table in its permanent design collection. Gray granted worldwide rights to manufacture her designs to Aram Designs Ltd., London.

RONALD A. GRIMALDI designed the Rogers Memorial Library Designers Showcase, South Hampton, NY. He has been published in numerous interior design magazines. The Rose Cumming firm was begun in 1917 by Rose Cumming and has been in constant operation since then.

Rose Cumming
232 East 59th Street
New York, NY 10022
Tel: 212-758-0844
Fax: 212-888-2837
Web site: www.rosecumming.com

ALBERT HADLEY is regarded as America's preeminent interior decorator. He has been heralded by the national and international press as the dean of interior design. His roster of clients includes presidents of the United States, the vice president, American ambassadors, distinguished individuals, and families. He is a member of the Interior Design Hall of Fame and a fellow of ASID and has honorary degrees from Parsons and The New York School of Design.

Following his career at McMillen, Inc., Hadley and Mrs. Henry Parish II founded Parish-Hadley, Inc. in 1962. That company closed its offices in 1999. Albert Hadley Inc. was opened in 2000. Archives of Hadley's work are held at the Cooper-Hewitt National Design Museum.

Hadley's work is defined by his keen sense of architectural detail and proportion. His careful use of color and form exemplifies a strong sense of editing. His goal is to help his clients realize more than they thought possible within the framework of their own taste.

Albert Hadley
24 East 64th Street
New York, NY 10021
Tel: 212-888-7979
Fax: 212-888-5597

ASHLEY HICKS was born in London in 1963. He studied fine art at Bath Academy of Art, and architecture at the Architectural Association, London. He has authored *David Hicks Designer* (Scriptum Editions, 2003).

ALLEGRA TONDATO HICKS was born in 1961 in Turin, Italy. She studied design at Politecnico di Milano and at Cooper Union in New York, and painting at the École van der Kelen in Brussels.

Ashley and Allegra were married in 1990 in Oxfordshire and honeymooned in India. They lived in New York in 1991–1992 and since then in London. They have two daughters.

Allegra designs rugs, furnishing and fashion fabrics, and fashion. In 2002, she opened the Allegra Hicks fashion outlet in Chelsea Green, London. Ashley designs architecture, furniture, accessories, and jewelry. Together they design interiors. The couple has authored *Design Alchemy* (Conran Octopus, 2002.)

Ashley & Allegra Hicks Studio
266 Fulham Road
London SW10 9EL
Tel: 020-7376-3939
Web site: www.allegrahicks.com

DAVID HICKS (1929–1998) was born in Coggeshall, Essex, U.K. He studied art and design at the Central School in London. In 1960, he married Lady Pamela Mountbatten. The couple lived in London and Oxfordshire with their two daughters and one son. Hicks designed interiors for private and commercial clients around the world, including Vidal Sassoon, Helena Rubinstein, Stanley Donen, John Schlesinger, the Prince of Wales, and the King of Saudi Arabia. He also designed fabrics, carpets, wallpapers, bed linens, accessories, jewelry, furniture, and gardens. His books include *David Hicks on Decoration* (Leslie Frewin, 1966); *David Hicks on Living—With Taste* (Leslie Frewin, 1968); *David Hicks on Bathrooms* (Britwell, 1970); *David Hicks on Decoration—With Fabrics* (Britwell, 1971); *David Hicks on Decoration—5* (Britwell, 1971); *Living with Design* (Weidenfeld & Nicholson, 1979); and *My Kind of Garden* (Garden Art Press, 1999).

THOMAS JAYNE established his interior design company, Thomas Jayne Studio, in 1990. He is often described as a historicist with a strong interest in American, English, and French styles; however, in practice his work covers a spectrum of styles and embraces a modern approach to decorating. Particular attention is paid in his work to presenting art and antique furniture collections; architectural planning and detailing; historical research; and color selection. The end results are rooms that speak to the past yet have a modern edge and sense of comfort appropriate to our times.

Thomas Jayne received a bachelor of arts in art history from the University of Oregon and completed graduate fellowships in the history of American decorative art and architecture at the Winterthur Museum Program in Early American Culture and at the American Wing of the Metropolitan Museum of Art in New York. He has been featured in *House Beautiful*'s 2002 list of Top 100 Designers and *New York Magazine*'s "The City's 100 Best Architects and Decorators" in 2002. He was selected in 1999 to be *Town & Country*'s first Showhouse designer, a periodic feature in which a single designer completes the decoration of a new house for a hypothetical client. Illustrations of Jayne's work have been published extensively; a sampling can be seen at www.thomasjaynestudio.com.

Thomas Jayne Studio
136 East 57th Street, #1704
New York, NY 10022
Tel: 212-838-9080/4751
Fax: 212-838-9654
e-mail: tjayne@thomasjaynestudio.com

JED JOHNSON (1948–1996) was born in 1948 in Minnesota. On a semester break from college in California, Jed and his twin brother Jay came to New York. Jed met Andy Warhol and became an employee of the Factory. He assisted director Paul Morrissey on films while he "helped Andy with his house"—a neoclassical cache of extraordinary collections. Yves St. Laurent and Pierre Bergé were impressed and asked Jed to do a Manhattan pied-à-terre. Peter and Sandra Brant, publishers of *Interview*, called and suddenly Jed had a new profession.

His partner for 18 years was architect Alan Wanzenberg. They collaborated on numerous projects that embodied the beautifully detailed and highly customized interiors that became his trademark. Johnson's residential commissions in America and Europe ran the stylistic gamut from period opulence to twentieth-century eclecticism. Clients included Mick Jagger and Carl Icahn.

Jed Johnson died in 1996 on TWA flight 800. His work, his beloved dachshunds, and his family—in particular his twin brother Jay—were his great passions. His work has appeared in a vast array of international design periodicals such as *Architectural Digest, House & Garden, House Beautiful,* and *Elle Decor* as well as many books including *Bathrooms, Bedrooms, The Curtain Design,* and *Adirondack Style.*

PAULINE C. METCALF combines a career as both an interior decorator and an architectural historian. She was the primary author for *Ogden Codman and The Decoration of Houses* (Athenaeum, 1988) and contributed the chapter on the interiors of David Adler and his sister, the interior decorator Frances Elkins, to *David Adler: The Elements of Style* (Art Institute of Chicago, 2002), the publication and exhibition sponsored by the Art Institute of Chicago. She has lectured widely and written for numerous publications. She has continued to research the role and influence of women decorators and collectors in the first half of the twentieth century, which she hopes will be a future publication.

Pauline Metcalf
19 East 88th Street
New York, NY 10128
Tel: 212-831-2486
Fax: 212-410-2899

JUAN PABLO MOLYNEUX was born in Santiago, Chile. He studied architecture at the Catholic University in Santiago and continued his architectural studies at the École des Beaux Arts in Paris. He also studied egyptology at the École du Louvre.

By the age of 27, Molyneux had already earned a reputation as one of the top interior designers in Chile. He was awarded a one-man show at the Museo National de Bellas Artes. In 1976, Molyneux and his wife, Pilar, relocated to Buenos Aires, Argentina. There, he reestablished his business and

continued winning prestigious clients throughout South America, Europe, and the United States. In 1982, he opened a second office in New York City to work more closely with his North American clientele. After a short time, Mr. and Mrs. Molyneux moved permanently to New York, to their current location in a six-story limestone townhouse on the fashionable Upper East Side. In 1997 Molyneux opened a satellite office in Paris.

Molyneux has lectured extensively in both North and South America. His work has been published in *Architectural Digest* over 20 times, as well as in a variety of other prestigious publications and book features. His monograph, *Molyneux,* was published by Rizzoli International Publication in the fall of 1997 and was launched in Paris, London, and New York. He and his work are featured extensively in the compendium "Americas Elite 1000"—The Ultimate List.

Molyneux is an avid snow skier and also quite passionate about his collection of Harley-Davidson motorcycles.

Juan Pablo Molyneux
29 East 69th Street
New York, NY 10021
Tel: 212-628-0097
Fax: 212-737-6126

RENZO MONGIARDINO (1916–1998) was enormously influenced by the Genoa palazzo where he was born on May 12, 1916, and where he lived with his parents until the mid-1930s. In 1936, Mongiardino went to Milan to study architecture under the direction of the renowned Modernist architect Giò Ponti. Driven by a strong understanding of and love for classical architecture, Mongiardino extended and adapted antique and Renaissance ideas from Vitruvius and Alberti to the lifestyles and needs of those who commissioned his work. A very close friend of the celebrated painter and art director Lila de Nobili, he created projects for set and stage designing. His clients, among the most important and renowned in the world, from the financial, intellectual, and social elites, commissioned Mongiardino to create stunning rooms for their homes. Mongiardino died in Milan on January 11, 1998.

JUAN MONTOYA was born and spent his early years in Bogotá, Colombia. He studied architecture at the Universidad Gran Colombia in Bogotá and environmental design at the Parsons School of Design in New York City. After working as an interior designer in Paris and Milan, he returned to New York City and opened his own office in 1978. His firm specializes in residential and contract interior design, with projects located in various parts of the United States as well as abroad. He also designs and markets an extensive line of furniture through Juan Montoya Furniture and Accessories. His work is very well publicized and appears frequently in both national and international publications.

In addition to his own work, Montoya lectures throughout the United States and abroad on various topics of design. The numerous awards he has received include the S. M. Hexter Award for Interior of the Year, the Chicago Design Sources Award for Excellence in the Field of Residential Interior Design, and the Resources Council Inc. Award for Furniture Design. Montoya was also honored by being chosen a panel member for the National Endowment of the Arts. In addition, he has been elected into the Interior Design Hall of Fame.

Juan Montoya
330 East 59th Street—2nd Floor
New York, NY 10022
Tel: 212-421-2400
Fax: 212-421-6240

SISTER PARISH (1901–1994), born into a prominent family in New York City, Mrs. Henry Parish II (Sister Parish) used her social contacts to establish her business during the Depression. Albert Hadley joined her in 1962, creating the legendary Parish-Hadley, Inc. Parish is credited with inventing the American country look—combining comfortable upholstered sofas, pillows, chintzes, soft rugs, antiques, pastel-colored walls, and bouquets of flowers.

As she herself said: "Innovation is often the ability to reach into the past and bring back what is good, what is beautiful, what is useful, what is lasting."

ROBERTO PEREGALLI and Laura Sartori Rimini carry on a unique architectural activity, with the collaboration of a number of craftsmen and decorators. Their work is particularly notable and appreciated because, while looking back with nostalgia at the past, it creates an atmosphere of illusion projected onto the future. Connection with past styles, love for individual objects, curiosity about the different expressions of art and history, and a personal concept of interior decoration are all aspects that are particularly dear to Roberto Peregalli, a pupil of Renzo Mongiardino's ever since the beginning, and to Laura Sartori Rimini, who has a degree in architecture from the University of Florence, specializing in the field of restoration.

The studio began activity in 1986 and carried out projects in the main locations in Europe, in addition to creating opera scenes and museum exhibitions. Their numerous projects have been published in renowned European and U.S. publications.

Studio Peregalli
Via Passione 11
20122 Milano
Tel/Fax: 0039-02-76014140

SUZANNE RHEINSTEIN was born and reared in the South. Her career as a designer grew from an interest in architecture and the decorative arts and a fascination with how people lived. Originally a journalist, for 15 years she has owned Hollyhock, a design store selling antiques, upholstered furniture, books, and unusual art and objects for decorating a house.

In the fall of 2002, Hollyhock moved to a former studio of Tony Duquette's in West Hollywood. At the same time, the design firm took on a new name, Suzanne Rheinstein and Associates. The firm's projects have recently included a Colonial-style farmhouse in the Virginia horse country, a new adobe in the shadows of the Sandia Mountains of New Mexico, a fashion designer's glamorous New York apartment, Florida retreats, a modernist high rise co-op in Los Angeles, and numerous family houses up and down the Southern California coast.

Suzanne Rheinstein & Associates
817 Hilldale Avenue
West Hollywood, CA 90069
Tel: 310-550-8900
Fax: 310-550-5864

JEAN ROYÈRE (1902–1981) is one of the most important French designers of the mid-twentieth century. His furniture, lamp, and textile designs and aesthetic have become iconic—the chevron or the sinusoid with its biomorphic shapes, from the "Elephanteau" armchair to the "Liane" floor lamp. "In art as in the military life, it is sometimes essential to disobey and take a risk. To transgress time with other rules is sometimes more advantageous than to strictly apply the theory a dozen times." Royère retired to Pennsylvania.

BETTY SHERRILL, a native of New Orleans, attended Newcomb College from 1940 to 1944, and in 1949 she attended the Parsons School of Design in New York City. In 1951, she became the assistant to the president of McMillen Inc. and was appointed as the president and chief executive officer in 1975. Today, she continues to serve as the chairman of McMillen.

She has served as vice president of the Boys Club of New York and as officer and member of the board of directors of the National Trust of New York State, as well as a member of the boards of Southampton Hospital and Memorial Sloan Kettering Hospital. She has been active in fund raising for these institutions over periods ranging from 5 to 25 years. She has also been a member of the National Foundation for Facial Reconstruction for 20 years.

Sherrill has maintained a close association with Tulane University, where she received her honorary doctorate degree as Outstanding Alumna of the Year in 1987. She is interested in the development of pro-

fessional education in the field of interior design and is currently working on a project to fund a joint degree program at Tulane between the School of Architecture and the art department. She is also a member of the board of trustees of Loyola University. Sherrill has received numerous honors and lectures extensively.

Betty Sherrill
McMillen Inc.
155 East 56th Street
New York, NY 10022
Tel: 212-753-5600
Fax: 212-759-7563

MARJORIE SHUSHAN, who is primarily self-taught, has been involved in interior design for 35 years. Her career began when she lived in New Orleans and designed an office as a favor, and she has been working ever since. After meeting Kalef Alaton in Aspen, she went to work with him in Los Angeles, and, as his East Coast commissions increased, she moved to New York as his representative. Since Kalef's death Marjorie has been operating her own firm, with numerous projects across the country. Published nine times in *Architectural Digest,* Marjorie has been on the *AD*100 list since 1995.

Marjorie Shushan
15 West 53rd Street
New York, NY 10019
Tel: 212-975-1200
Fax: 212-975-0097
e-mail: mshushaninc@aol.com

SIR JOHN SOANE (1753–1837), the son of a bricklayer, entered the Royal Academy School in 1771. In 1809 Soane became professor of architecture at the Royal Academy. He was knighted in 1832, and in 1833 he obtained an Act of Parliament through which his private house became a national architecture museum (the Sir John Soane's Museum, 13 Lincoln's Inn Fields, London, WC2A 3BP). One of England's greatest architects, he was responsible for the Bank of England; the Royal Hospital, Chelsea; the

Dulwich Picture Gallery; and interiors at the prime minister's residence at No. 10 Downing Street.

WILLIAM SOFIELD received his degree in architecture and urban planning from Princeton University in 1983, following an academic focus on art history and European cultural studies. The following September he received the Helena Rubenstein Fellowship from the Whitney Museum of American Art, which he received again the following year. Sofield first established his design practice in 1989, and in 1992 he cofounded Aero Studios. Studio Sofield, Inc., the interdisciplinary design workshop, was established in New York's SoHo district in 1996. The Los Angeles satellite office was created in 1999 to provide more extensive design services to West Coast and international clients. Studio Sofield's portfolio ranges from landscape design to residential, from retail to corporate office space design, and from hospitality to furniture design.

William Sofield lectures at numerous schools and universities and is a Fellow of the Frick Collection. He donates design services and strategic support to numerous nonprofit organizations, including the Brooklyn Academy of Music, The Whitney Museum of American Art, the Whitney Independent Study Program, The Parrish Museum, the Merchant's House Museum, the Irvington Institute for Medical Research, the Alzheimer's Association, AIDS Project Los Angeles, DIFFA, and CRIA.

William Sofield
Studio Sofield, Inc.
380 Lafayette Street, PH2
New York City, NY 10003
Tel: 212-473-1300
Fax: 212-473-0300
e-mail: design@studiosofield.com

PHILIPPE STARCK (1949–) was born in Paris. He designed the interiors of the nightclubs of La Main Bleue (1976) and Les Bains-Douche (1978) in Paris and in 1979 founded the company Starck Product. He refurbished private apartments in the Elysée Palace (1982) for President François Mitterand of France; the Maison Lemoult (1987); the La Flamme building (1989) in Tokyo; the Nani Nani office building (1989); an entire street block, Rue Starck (1991), in Paris, Café Costes in Paris; the Royalton and Paramount hotels in New York; the Delano in Miami; and the Mondrian in Los Angeles. He also designs furniture and domestic items for mass production.

JOHN STEFANIDIS was born in Egypt and educated at Oxford University. In 1967 he started his London-based interior design practice in Chelsea. He has designed for clients around the world. He is the author of *Rooms: Design and Decoration* (Cassell, 2002) and *Living by Design: Creating Atmosphere, Effect and Comfort* (Weidenfeld & Nicholson, 1997). He lives in London and spends time at his house on the Greek Island of Patmos.

John Stefanidis
St. John's Parish Hall
374 North End Road
London SW6 1LY
Tel: 44-20-738-11311
Fax: 44-207-610-2348
e-mail: martin@stefanidis.co.uk

MICHAEL TAYLOR (1927–1986) was born in Modesto, California, and educated at the Rudolf Schaeffer School of Interior Design in San Francisco. He was influenced by Syrie Maugham (1879–1955) and acquired most of Francis Elkins's business estate when she died, including designs bought from Syrie Maugham. He formed a partnership with Francis Mihailoff in 1952. He liked using color but not a multitude of colors in the same room; semitropical plants; and using a single pattern throughout a room. In 1956 he opened his own business. In 1985 he founded Michael Taylor Designs with Paul Weaver. He died of AIDS at the age of 59.

EMILIO TERRY (1890–1969), a Cuban-born architect and designer, was self educated and was was greatly influenced by the Château de Chenonceau,

Nicolas Ledoux, the Palladio, and the style of Louis XVI. In 1934 Terry repurchased the castle of Rochecotte (Saint-Patrice) from his brother-in-law. Clients included Charles de Beistegui (Chateau de Groussay), Prince Rainer of Monaco, and Niarchos. Terry is also known for his furniture designs.

CARLETON VARNEY, one of America's best known interior designers, is also a well-known syndicated newspaper columnist and the author of more than 20 books. He was the design consultant to the Carter Presidential Library and for numerous functions at the White House. In years past, he restored and redecorated the official vice president's residence in Washington, DC; the governor's mansion in West Virginia; and the U.S. Embassy in Tokyo, and is associated with the restoration and decoration of countless hotels and resorts all over the world, among them Dromoland and Ashford Castles in Ireland, the Waldorf Towers and the Plaza Hotel in New York, the Grand Hotel on Mackinac Island, The Breakers in Palm Beach, and the Greenbrier Hotel in West Virginia.

Varney's versatility in design can be seen in the wide range of products that bear his mark, including furniture, lamps, dinnerware, crystal, and linen designs. His own line of fabric designs, launched under the name Carleton Varney by the Yard, graces the private residences of his impressive roster of clients, which includes superstars from the worlds of entertainment, fashion, and business. He has a design and sales office in Sarasota, Florida, and a design office/boutique in Newmarket-on-Fergus, County Clare, Ireland. He is the president of Dorothy Draper & Co. Inc. of New York, the oldest established interior design firm in the United States, named after the founder of the company, who was one of the doyennes of interior design from the 1920s to the 1960s.

Carleton Varney
Dorothy Draper & Co. Inc.
60 East 56th Street
New York, NY 10022
Tel: 212-758-2810
Fax: 212-759-0739

EDITH WHARTON (1862–1937) broke through the strictures of her tightly controlled upbringing to become one of America's greatest writers. Author of *The House of Mirth, The Age of Innocence,* and *Ethan Frome,* she wrote more than 40 books in 40 years, including authoritative works on architecture and interior design, landscape gardening, and travel. Essentially self-educated, she was the first woman awarded the Pulitzer Prize for Fiction, an honorary doctorate of letters from Yale University, and full membership in the American Academy of Arts and Letters.

Wharton's 1902 home—The Mount in Lenox, Massachusetts—was her design laboratory where she implemented the principles articulated in her first major book, *The Decoration of Houses* (1897). Wharton believed that the design of a house should be treated architecturally and should honor the principles of proportion, harmony, simplicity, and suitability. She viewed proportion as the "good breeding of architecture" and symmetry as the "sanity of decoration." She saw house decoration as "a branch of architecture" and the decorator's role as "not to explain illusions, but to produce them." She thought gardens, too, should be architectural compositions. She wrote in *Italian Villas and Their Gardens* that gardens should be divided into rooms and planned in concert with the house and the natural landscape.

Wharton moved to France in 1911. She died there on the eve of World War II.

BUNNY WILLIAMS opened her own firm, Bunny Williams Incorporated, in 1988, after 22 years with the venerable decorating firm Parish-Hadley Associates. Restraint and appropriateness are hallmarks of the classically schooled Williams's style. Objects, patterns, textures, and colors, beautifully balanced, have an appealing, undisciplined look—the direct result of great focus and meticulous planning.

Williams was inducted into the Interior Design Hall of Fame in 1996. She was also awarded the prestigious Design and Business Award by the Edith Wharton Restoration. She was included in *House*

Beautiful's Top 100 in November 2002. Williams is on the board of directors of the Lenox Hill Neighborhood House, the Garden Conservancy, the Institute of Classical Architecture, the Humane Society of New York, and Tails in Need, Inc. Today her design work is regularly featured in design magazines such as *House & Garden, House Beautiful, Architectural Digest, Veranda, Elle Decor, Victoria, British House & Garden,* and *Garden Design.*

Bunny Williams
306 East 61st Street, Fifth Floor
New York, New York 10021
Tel: 212-207-4040
Fax: 212-207-4353
e-mail: haleystevenson@bunnywilliamsinc.com

RON WILSON began designing when he was 26 years old. His scholastic background is limited to a high school degree with no formal training in design. His work has been featured in *Architectural Digest, House & Garden, House Beautiful,* and magazines throughout the world. He has been named one of *Architectural Digest*'s 100 best designers and has lectured on design at the Smithsonian Institution, UCLA, and USC. Wilson is proud to sponsor the Ron Wilson Art Gallery at Pepperdine University in Malibu, California, which features the work of fine contemporary artists in a beautiful space.

At Ron Wilson Designer, the small office staff gives very personal attention to clients. The firm is known for doing all types of interiors including Italian, Asian, English, and contemporary styles. Ron Wilson Designer has had a varied clientele including both commercial and residential projects. Commercial projects have included banks, country clubs, and medical offices. Residential clients have included Michael Landon, Johnny Carson, Tom Selleck, Kenny Rogers, and Cher. Ron Wilson has a line of furniture aptly named The Ron Wilson Collection.

Ron Wilson Design
1235 Tower Road
Beverly Hills, CA 90210
Tel: 310-276-0666
Fax: 310-276-7291
e-mail: www.ronwilsondesigner.com

VICENTE WOLF has been at the top of the world of contemporary design for 28 years. He heads his own company, Vicente Wolf Associates in New York City, where he has designed a wide range of projects including the Luxe Hotel Rodeo Drive in Beverly Hills; L'Impero Restaurant in New York; the executive offices of J records for Clive Davis; and the New York City apartment of Mr. and Mrs. Michael Lynne, president of New Line Cinema. He is presently designing a restaurant and retail store for Steve Wynn's new hotel Le Reve in Las Vegas. An accomplished photographer, he has had several one-man shows and his work appears in *Elle Decor, House Beautiful, Architectural Digest, Veranda, The New York Times Magazine* and numerous other publications. Artisan just published Wolf's first book, *Learning to See.*

Vicente Wolf's VW Home showroom carries everything for the home, including antique furniture and accessories. VW Home also features furniture, upholstery, lighting, fabrics, wallpaper, and mirrors designed by Wolf.

Vicente Wolf
333 West 39th Street
New York, NY 10018
Tel: 212-465-0590

ABOUT THE EDITOR

Susan Gray is a people and portrait photographer and writer. She has worked with a number of major corporations, magazines, and museums. The Eastman Kodak Company sponsored her first book, *Writers on Directors* (Foreword by Leonard Maltin), and her critically acclaimed second title, *Architects on Architects* (Foreword by Paul Goldberger), was sponsored by USG Corporation and reviewed in major publications including *The New York Times Book Review* (a "revealing . . . collection") as well as *Publisher's Weekly* ("architects and enthusiasts will delight in this moving erudite collection").